The Giant Book of Bulletin Boards

Editor
Joellyn Thrall Cicciarelli

Illustrator
Darcy Tom

Designer
Moonhee Pak

Project Director
Carolea Williams

Contributing Writers

Patricia Albright	Kellie Hicks
Sarah Bailey	Ronda Howley
Nancy Barry	Catherine Johnson
Judith Boufford	Amy Kaser
Teresa Catta-Preta	Renee Keeler
Kim Cernek	Jonna Kupchik
Lucia Corsaro	Mary Kurth
Marilyn Donoho	Margaret Maxwell
Adela Garcia	Kathy McKee
Donna Hankinson	Susan Murphy
Elaine Hansen	Magi Oka
Dorothy Hewitt	Terry Peterson

Table of Contents

Here they are—the best bulletin boards created by the best teachers! Teachers from all over the United States and abroad have contributed their favorite ideas to make *The Giant Book of Bulletin Boards* your one-stop resource for a beautiful, engaging learning environment.

 And because *The Giant Book of Bulletin Boards* was developed by real teachers in real classrooms, everything you need is here. Take a look. . . .

With each bulletin board idea, you'll find

✪ a delightful illustration that shows exactly what the board will look like

✪ a materials list of readily available supplies

✪ a detailed explanation of how to make the board

✪ reproducible patterns for large and small images

✪ background color suggestions

✪ coordinating border ideas (described on book pages and displayed in full color on the inside back cover)

✪ paper cut-out suggestions (described on book pages and displayed in full color on the inside front cover)

✪ "another idea"—an alternate title or subject

 And it doesn't stop there! After using the dozens of reproducible patterns for your bulletin boards, you can use them to enhance student learning and create a coordinated look or theme. You can use the patterns in a myriad of ways, such as for door and window decorations, book-making activities, art projects, story-writing stationery, or puppets. In addition, board-making tips are presented on page 5 to help you design and preserve your bulletin boards for lasting appeal.

 Because of the abundant ideas and patterns, your classroom will look fresh and exciting month after month, year after year. So flip through the book, choose your favorite bulletin boards, and start decorating! You and your students will be thrilled with the results.

Board-Making Tips

 Try some of the following ideas to make your bulletin boards attractive, exciting, and durable.

✪ Enlarge bulletin-board pages and reproducibles using transparencies and an overhead projector, for easy tracing onto butcher paper.

✪ Stuff large images for a 3-D effect, or glue on tissue-paper squares for texture.

✪ Enhance large images with 3-D embellishments, such as glitter, plastic flowers, raffia, or yarn.

✪ Fold, shape, weave, and crinkle butcher-paper images and backgrounds to give your boards realistic, eye-catching effects.

✪ For interesting backgrounds, use fabric, corrugated paper, or newspaper.

✪ Experiment with painting and coloring techniques on large images and back-grounds. For example, paint splatters look like rain or snow and "crayon-resist" gives an underwater look. Finger-painting and sponge-painting add interest as well.

✪ To hide uneven background edges, use matching borders to line the perimeter of your boards. Coordinating borders are suggested throughout the book. Consult the inside back cover for more information about obtaining them.

✪ Use ready-made paper cut-outs to save assembly time. Large and small precut paper cut-outs in two colors are suggested throughout the book. Consult the inside front cover for more information about obtaining them.

✪ For headings, use purchased, die-cut, hand-printed (by children), stamped, or sponge-painted letters.

✪ Laminate entire boards for use year after year.

✪ File your boards in a large box or cupboard according to season or month. Create a master list for reference and post it on the box or cupboard. Then pack the boards so they always look new.

Whether you reproduce the bulletin boards exactly or add your own personal flair, *The Giant Book of Bulletin Boards* offers everything you need. Get started today!

Come On In for a Bushel of Fun!

 Cut a large "bushel basket" from tan butcher paper. Tape the basket near the top of your door so the basket is angled upside down. Write a student's name on each construction-paper apple cut-out. Tape the apples to the door so they look like they are falling out of the basket. Tape the headline *Come On In for a Bushel of Fun!* at the top of your door.

MATERIALS

- ✪ tan butcher paper
- ✪ red, green, or yellow construction-paper apple cut-outs

Another Idea: Change the title to *You're the Apple of My Eye!*
Red/Green Apple Cut-Outs (CTP 4884)

Blue background ♣ Kids of the World border (CTP 0143)

Take a Peek at Your Class!

Have each child decorate a paper plate to represent his or her face. Invite students to trace their hands onto construction paper and cut out the handprints. Ask each student to write his or her first name on the inside of the right hand and his or her last name on the inside of the left hand. Ask students to glue each hand to a side of the paper-plate face. Staple the faces to the bulletin board and fold in the hands so they cover the faces. Add the title *Take a Peek at Your Class!* Invite students to visit the board and open the hands to see their classmates.

 **MATERIALS**

✪ paper plates
✪ art supplies
✪ construction paper

Another Idea: Substitute a student's name for *Our Class*, and invite a "student of the week" to write information about himself or herself on paper stars.

Red background ❖ Gold Stars border (CTP 0151) ❖ Blue/Yellow Star Cut-Outs (CTP 4896)

Our Class, Starring . . .

Enlarge, trace, color, and cut out the Movie Camera. Staple the camera to the center of the bulletin board. Glue or tape each student's photo to the center of a paper star cut-out. Trace the perimeter of each star with glue and sprinkle glitter on the glue. Hang the stars around the camera. Add the title *Our Class, Starring. . . .*

 **MATERIALS**

✪ Movie Camera (page 164)

✪ paper star cut-outs

✪ student photos

✪ glitter

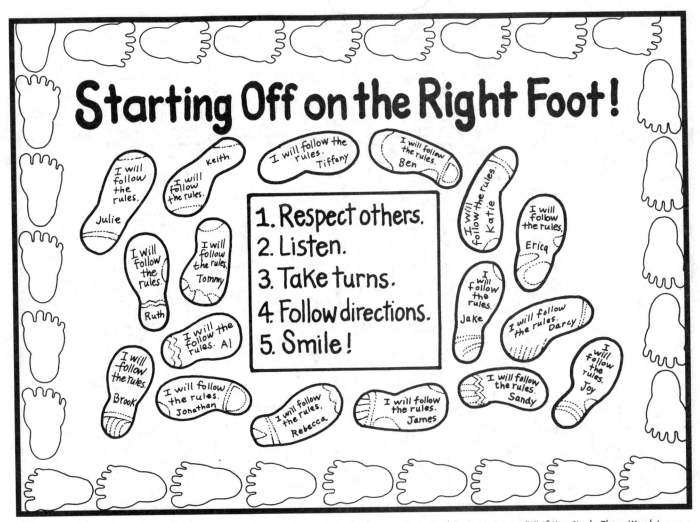

Another Idea: Write weekly spelling words on the poster and change the heading to *You're a Shoe-in to Get an "A" If You Study These Words!*

Green background ❖ Brown/Tan Footprint Cut-Outs used as border (CTP 4865)

Starting Off on the Right Foot!

Attach a poster with your classroom rules in the center of a bulletin board. Label the bulletin board *Starting Off on the Right Foot!* Invite each student to bring in an old shoe. Have students paint the bottom of the shoe and stamp it on construction paper. When the paint is dry, ask students to write on the shoe print *I will follow the rules*. Then have them sign the shoe print. Invite students to cut out the shoe prints and staple them to the board.

 **MATERIALS**

✪ poster of classroom rules
✪ old shoes brought from home
✪ tempera paint/paintbrushes

Another Idea: Change the heading to *It's Going to Be a "Grape" Year!*
Yellow background

We Make a Great Bunch!

Write each student's name on a purple construction-paper circle. Attach the circles to make a "bunch of grapes." Cut three or four large "grape leaves" from green butcher paper and staple them above the bunch of grapes. Curl green butcher-paper strips around a pencil to make spirals and attach them to the leaves. Write *We Make a Great Bunch!* on a purple butcher-paper strip and staple it on top of the leaves. Tape a student photo on each "grape."

 **MATERIALS**

✪ *purple construction-paper circles*

✪ *green butcher paper*

✪ *purple butcher-paper strip*

✪ *student photos*

Another Idea: Change the heading to *You're Important to Our Team. We Couldn't Bear It without You!*

Blue background ✤ Brown Bears border (CTP 0132) ✤ Brown/Red Bear Cut-Outs (CTP 4899)

We Make a "Beary" Good Team!

Enlarge, trace, color, and cut out the Bear. Staple the bear to the center of a bulletin board titled *We Make a "Beary" Good Team!* Attach a plastic whistle necklace and a folded baseball cap to the bear. Write a student's name on each paper bear cut-out. Invite each student to use art supplies to design a baseball cap for his or her bear and glue it to the bear. Staple the bears around the "coach."

 **MATERIALS**

✪ Bear (page 165)

✪ plastic whistle necklace

✪ baseball cap

✪ paper bear cut-outs

✪ art supplies

Brown and Light Blue background (see activity directions) ✤ Brown/Tan Boy Cut-Outs (CTP 4867) ✤ Brown/Tan Girl Cut-Outs (CTP 4868)

Welcome Aboard!

Staple light-blue butcher paper on a bulletin board as a background. Staple a brown butcher paper "hill" over the background. Enlarge, trace, color, and cut out the engine and several rail cars from the Train reproducible. Staple the sides and bottoms of the engine and rail cars to a bulletin board titled *Welcome Aboard!* Link the cars with strands of yarn. Write a student's name on each paper boy or girl cut-out and slip two cut-outs in each rail car. Write your name on a cut-out and place it in the engine.

 **MATERIALS**

- ✪ light-blue and brown butcher paper
- ✪ Train (page 166)
- ✪ paper boy and girl cut-outs
- ✪ yarn

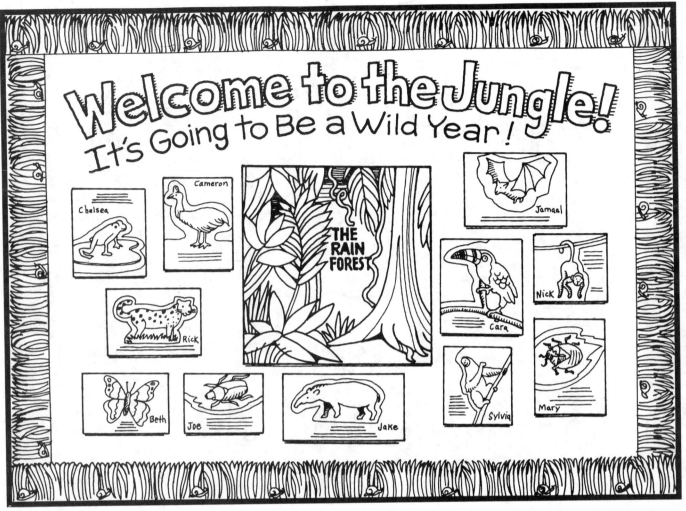

Yellow background ♣ Grass border (CTP 0359)

Welcome to the Jungle!

Staple a poster of a "rain forest scene" to the center of a bulletin board. Give each student a magazine or calendar picture of a rain forest animal and invite him or her to compare the animal in the picture to himself or herself. Ask students to use black marker to write on the picture their name and one thing they have in common with the animal. For example, a student may write *I am like a parrot because I like to talk*. Staple the pictures around the rain forest scene and add the title *Welcome to the Jungle! It's Going to Be a Wild Year!*

 **MATERIALS**

- ✪ poster of a "rain forest scene"
- ✪ magazine or calendar pictures of rain forest animals
- ✪ black markers

Green background ♣ Grass border (CTP 0359)

Teeing Off to a Great Year!

Cut out a white construction-paper circle (golf ball) for each student. Write students' names in the center of the balls. Cut out a large white butcher-paper "golf ball" for yourself and write your name on it. Attach the balls to the bulletin board, placing your ball in the center. Attach an upside down construction-paper triangle "tee" under each golf ball. Tape together a handful of plastic "grass" and staple it under each tee. Add the heading *Teeing Off to a Great Year!*

 **MATERIALS**

- ✪ white construction-paper circles
- ✪ white butcher paper
- ✪ construction-paper triangles
- ✪ plastic "grass"

Inside the illustration:
YOU'RE AN IMPORTANT PIECE IN OUR PUZZLE. WELCOME!

Katy
Jacob
Cecilia
Stanley
Jim
Sarah
Chuck
Peter
Sue

Dan
Cody
Patrick
Laurie
Cara
Morgan
Eddie
Darcy
Ben

Another Idea: Change the board to an incentive board. Each time the class is "caught being good," add a rectangle to the board. Treat the class when the mural is complete.

White Construction-Paper background (see activity directions)

You're an Important Piece . . .

Tape together several pieces of white construction paper (one piece per student) to make a rectangular "puzzle." Number the back of each paper in order. Write (in "bubble letters") *You're an Important Piece in Our Puzzle. Welcome!* in the center of the puzzle. Write each student's name (in "bubble letters") around the message. Take apart the puzzle and invite each student to decorate a rectangle and the letters inside it with crayons or markers. Have the class work together to assemble the puzzle. Then staple each rectangle to a bulletin board to make a colorful class mural.

 **MATERIALS**

✪ white construction paper

✪ art supplies

Another Idea: Each week, invite a student to decorate the board to tell about himself or herself.

Yellow background ✤ Red Apples border (CTP 0131)

All about Me

Have another teacher trace your body on black butcher paper. Cut around the body and staple it to a bulletin board titled *All about Me*. Print on index cards words that describe you and the things you enjoy. Attach the cards and favorite personal objects on and around the body cut-out. Use the board to introduce yourself the first day of school.

 **MATERIALS**

✪ *black butcher paper*

✪ *index cards*

✪ *favorite personal objects*

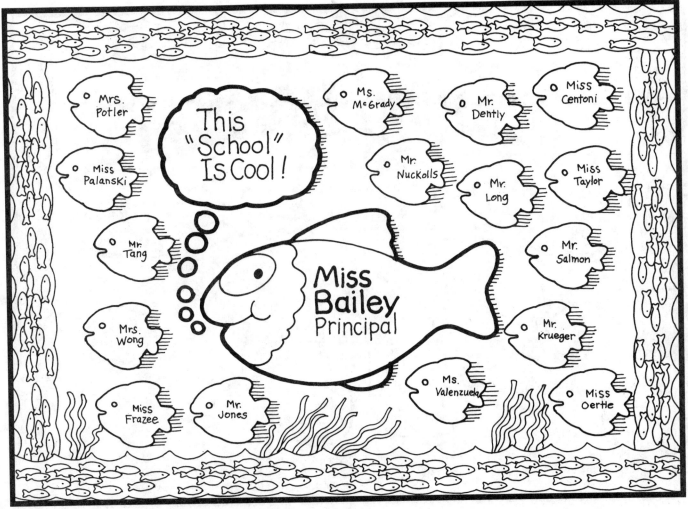

Another Idea: Write your name on the large fish and students' names on the small ones.

Light Blue background ✤ School of Fish border (CTP 0113) ✤ Gold/Blue Fish Cut-Outs (CTP 4874)

This "School" Is Cool!

Enlarge, trace, color, and cut out a Fish and staple it to the center of a blue bulletin board. Write the principal's name in the center of the fish. Write staff members' names on fish cut-outs (or Fish reproducible) and staple those fish on the board. Attach plastic grass "seaweed" and add the heading *This "School" Is Cool!*

 **MATERIALS**

❂ Fish (page 167)

❂ paper fish cut-outs or Fish (page 167)

❂ plastic grass

Another Idea: Change the title to *It Comes in Eights–Isn't That Great?* Write something that "comes in eights" on each clam, such as sides on an octagon or spider legs.

Light Blue background ✤ Under the Sea border (CTP 0114)

Helping Hands!

Enlarge, trace, color, and cut out the Octopus. Choose eight student-helper jobs and write each on the leg of the octopus. Staple the octopus to the center of a bulletin board titled *Helping Hands!* Reproduce a clam for each student, write a student's name on each clam, and cut out the clams. Put the clams in a plastic fishbowl that has been placed near the bulletin board. Choose eight clams each week and staple each clam to a different leg of the octopus to indicate student helpers.

 **MATERIALS**

✪ Octopus (page 168)
✪ Clams (page 169)
✪ plastic fishbowl

Yellow background ❧ Sunny Smiles border (CTP 0352) ❧ Blue/Yellow Star Cut-Outs (CTP 4896)

Happy to Help!

Title a bulletin board *Happy to Help!* Under the title, attach the following objects:

✪ eraser (chalkboard monitor)

✪ miniature flag (pledge leader)

✪ paper star cut-out (line leader)

✪ paper door (door holder)

✪ black plastic cup lined with a small plastic bag (garbage monitor)

✪ paper strips attached to the end of a straw (sweeper)

✪ kitchen rag (table cleaner)

✪ piece of notebook paper (paper monitor)

Label each item with its "job description." Place a tack under each item.

Write students' names on index cards and punch a hole in the center of each card. Every week, hang a different card on each tack.

 **MATERIALS**

✪ *"real-life" objects (see bulletin board description)*

✪ *hole punch*

✪ *index cards*

Another Idea: Change the heading to *Reading Is a Piece of Cake.* Invite students to write on cupcake liners titles of books they have read.
Purple background ✤ Birthday Cupcakes border (CTP 0133) ✤ Pink/Green Cupcake Cut-Outs (CTP 4898)

Happy Birthday, Cupcake!

Accordion-fold butcher paper to make a giant "cupcake liner." Attach a large butcher-paper "cupcake top" above the liner. Add a butcher-paper "candle" to the top of the cupcake and attach it to a bulletin board titled *Happy Birthday, Cupcake!* Attach twelve aluminum serving trays or pie tins around the cupcake. Label each tray with a month of the year. Write students' names on paper cupcake cut-outs and place each cut-out in the tray or pie tin that shows the month in which the student was born.

 **MATERIALS**

✪ butcher paper

✪ aluminum serving trays or pie tins

✪ paper cupcake cut-outs

Bear Hugs for Your Birthday!

January

April

July

October

February

May

August

November

March

June

September

December

Yellow background ✤ Brown Bears border (CTP 0132) ✤ Brown/Red Bear Cut-Outs (CTP 4899)

Bear Hugs for Your Birthday!

Write the name of each month on a different sentence strip and attach the strips around the perimeter of the bulletin board. Add the heading *Bear Hugs for Your Birthday!* Enlarge, trace, color, and cut out the Bear. Fold the bear's arms and staple the bear to the center of the bulletin board. Write each student's name on a paper bear cut-out and place each cut-out near the name of the month in which the student was born.

 **MATERIALS**

✪ Bear (page 165)

✪ paper bear cut-outs

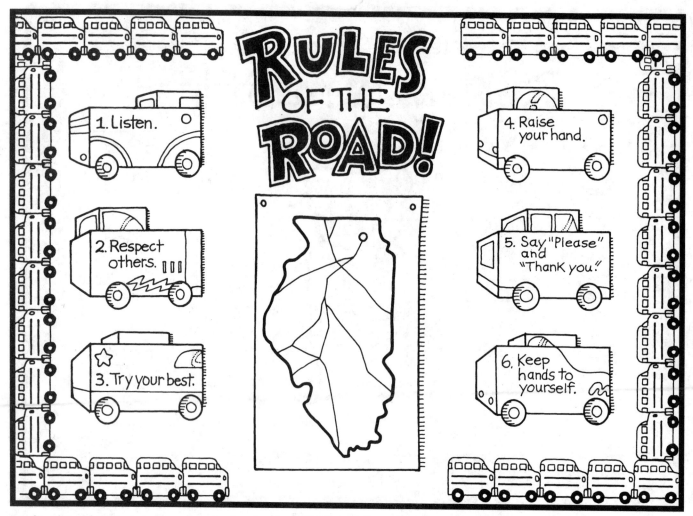

Another Idea: Change the board to an incentive board. Make small paper cars for student teams and "race them" from one point on the map to another as they show good behavior.

Blue background ♣ School Bus border (CTP 0152)

Rules of the Road!

Staple your state map in the center of a bulletin board titled *Rules of the Road!* Invite five or six student groups to use a shoe box and art supplies to design a car. Use black marker to write a class rule across the body of each car. Staple the cars on the bulletin board around the map.

 **MATERIALS**

- ✪ state map
- ✪ five or six shoe boxes
- ✪ art supplies
- ✪ black marker

Orange background ♣ Brown/Tan Footprint Cut-Outs (CTP 4865)

Step into (First) Grade!

Staple a brown butcher-paper "door" in the center of a bulletin board. Cover a small margarine lid with aluminum foil and attach it to the paper door as a doorknob. Invite students to write on a paper foot cut-out their name and an "action word" to complete the following sentence: *I'll put my best foot forward when I learn to (school activity) this year.* Surround the paper door with stapled-on feet. Add the heading *Step into (First) Grade!*

 **MATERIALS**

✪ *brown butcher-paper "door"*

✪ *small margarine lid*

✪ *aluminum foil*

✪ *paper foot cut-outs*

White background ✤ Sports border (CTP 0356)

Let's Reach Our Goals This Year!

Staple a square of fishing net to the center of a bulletin board. Draw "posts" from the net so it looks like a hockey net. Cut a large "hockey stick" from construction paper and staple it to the left of the net. Invite each student to cut out a "hockey puck" from black construction paper and write with chalk a goal he or she has for the year. Attach the pucks to the net with paper clips. Add the heading *Let's Reach Our Goals This Year!*

 **MATERIALS**

✪ *fishing net*

✪ *black construction paper*

✪ *chalk*

✪ *paper clips*

Another Idea: Invite students to write a story explaining what they think the Tooth Fairy does with the teeth after she collects them. Attach the stories to the bulletin board.

Dark Pink background ✤ Gold Stars border (CTP 0151) ✤ White/Pink Tooth Cut-Outs (CTP 4871)

Tooth Fairy Treasures

Enlarge, trace, color, and cut out the Tooth Fairy and her treasure chest. Staple the Tooth Fairy to the center of a bulletin board titled *Tooth Fairy Treasures*. Have each student write his or her name on a paper tooth cut-out. Attach the paper teeth to the bulletin board. As each student loses a tooth, move his or her tooth and staple it inside the Tooth Fairy's treasure chest. Continue moving tooth cut-outs throughout the year.

 **MATERIALS**

✪ Tooth Fairy (page 170)
✪ paper tooth cut-outs

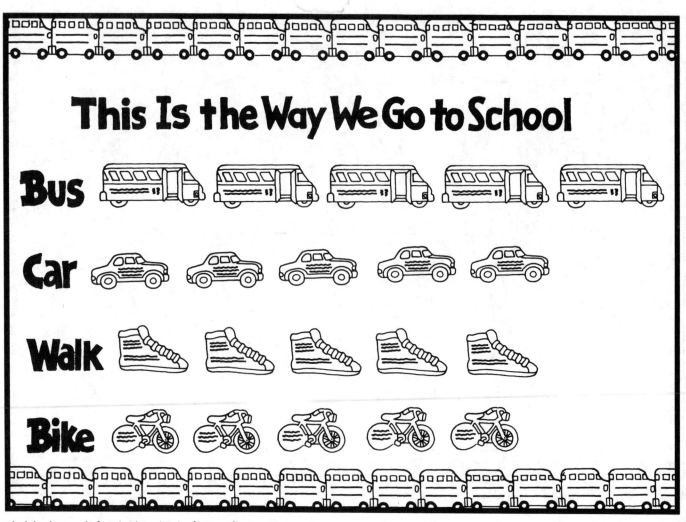

This Is the Way We Go to School

Bus

Car

Walk

Bike

Black background ♣ School Bus border (CTP 0152)

This Is the Way We Go to School

Divide a bulletin board into four horizontal sections. Label the first section *Bus,* the second *Car,* the third *Walk,* and the fourth *Bike.* Add the heading *This Is the Way We Go to School.* Ask students to decide how they usually go to school and color and cut out a Bus, Car, Shoe, or Bike to match their choice. Have "bus students" write their bus number on the bus; have "car students" write on the car who drops them off most often; and have the "shoe students" and "bike students" write on the shoe the name of their street. Invite students to attach their cut-outs to the board.

 MATERIALS

✪ Bus, Car, Shoe, and Bike (page 171)

"Fall" In for Some Fall Fun!

Write each student's name on an individual paper leaf cut-out. Staple the cut-outs to the door so they look like they are falling from a tree. Add the heading *"Fall" In for Some Fall Fun!*

MATERIALS

✪ *paper leaf cut-outs*

Another Idea: Attach the board to the inside of your door and change the heading to *Please Shut the Door When You "Leaf"!*

Red/Yellow Autumn Leaf Cut-Outs (CTP 4885)

Another Idea: Leave the board up all year and change the name at the beginning of each season. For winter, have students write poems on snowflake shapes; for spring, have them write poems on paper flowers; and for summer, have students write poems on green paper leaves.

Green background ✤ Maple Leaves border (CTP 0138) ✤ Red/Green Apple Cut-Outs (CTP 4884)

Fall Poet Tree

Twist brown butcher-paper strips to resemble a tree trunk and branches. Staple the "tree" to a bulletin board. Attach green paper leaves to the branches. Have each student write the following poem on a paper apple cut-out:

> *I am special.*
> *I am me.*
> *I can be anything I want to be.*
> *I want to be a*
>
> _____

Ask students to fill in the blank with an occupation they might like to have when they grow up. Attach the apples to the branches. Label the bulletin board *Fall Poet Tree*.

 **MATERIALS**

- ✪ brown butcher-paper strips
- ✪ green paper leaves
- ✪ paper apple cut-outs

DON'T BE SCARED OF COMPOUND WORDS!

hand shake

butterfly

basket ball

Seafood

race track

soft ball

quicksand

stop watch

Another Idea: Have students write math problems on the scarecrow arms and the answers on the chest. Change the heading to *We're Not Scared of Math!*

Yellow background ❖ Pumpkins border (CTP 0139)

Don't Be Scared of Compound Words!

Invite students to color and cut out a Scarecrow. Have each student use black permanent marker to write a compound word in the center of the scarecrow. Ask students to fold the scarecrow's arms on the dotted lines and color the other side of the arms to match the already colored clothing. Have students write the first half of the compound word on the left arm and the second half of the word on the right arm. Display the scarecrows on a bulletin board titled *Don't Be Scared of Compound Words!*

 **MATERIALS**

✪ Scarecrow (page 172)

✪ black permanent markers

Another Idea: Change the title to *Ho, Ho, Hope You Have a Nice Vacation!* Have students decorate the handprints like Santa Claus faces.
Black background (see activity directions) ❧ Pumpkins border (CTP 0139)

Flying By with a Halloween Hi!

Invite students to paint a hand white and press it upside down on a large black butcher-paper background. Invite students to paint two black "ghost eyes" on their handprints to turn them into ghosts. Use white paint to add the heading *Flying By with a Halloween Hi!* Attach the mural to a bulletin board.

 **MATERIALS**

✪ *white and black tempera paint/paintbrushes*

✪ *black butcher paper*

Another Idea: Attach student photos inside windows and doors and add the heading *Frightfully Fun Photos!*

Purple background ♣ Picket Fence border (CTP 0358)

Do the Math . . .

Enlarge, trace, color, and cut out the Haunted House. Cut the dotted lines on all the doors and windows so they open and close. Attach the house to a bulletin board and write a math equation (without the answer) on each door and window. Then open the doors and windows and write on the bulletin board background the answers to the problems. Add the heading *Do the Math if You Dare. Then Open Up to See What's There!* Invite students to visit the board, calculate an answer for each equation, and open the doors and windows to check their answers.

 **MATERIALS**

⭐ *Haunted House (page 173)*

Another Idea: Change the heading to *I Love My "Mummy"!* Have students draw portraits of their mothers or special female friends and attach them to the board.

Black background ✤ Pumpkins border (CTP 0139) ✤ Orange/Yellow Pumpkin Cut-Outs (CTP 4887)

Wrapped Up In Reading!

Trace and cut out a child's silhouette on white butcher paper to make a "mummy." Attach the mummy to the left side of a bulletin board and add the title *Wrapped Up In Reading!* Tape strands of bathroom tissue over the mummy so it appears to have real wrappings. Write students' names on paper pumpkin cut-outs. Scatter the pumpkins around the bulletin board. Invite each student to draw a picture of or write a book report about a favorite Halloween read-aloud book and hang each student's paper near his or her pumpkin.

 **MATERIALS**

❂ white butcher paper
❂ bathroom tissue
❂ paper pumpkin cut-outs
❂ pictures of or book reports about a favorite Halloween read-aloud

Another Idea: Have students write "bat facts" on the bats and change the heading to *Going Batty for Bats!*

Yellow background ✤ Black/Purple Halloween Bat Cut-Outs used as border (CTP 4872)

We're Batty about Contractions!

Reproduce on brown construction paper a Bat for each student. Have students cut out their bat and glue on two raisin "eyes." Invite each student to write a contraction on the bat's stomach and fold the bat wings on the dotted lines. Then have students write the "long version" of the contraction on the folded wings so one word is written on each wing. Attach the bats to a bulletin board titled *We're Batty about Contractions!*

 **MATERIALS**

✪ Bat (page 174)

✪ raisins

Another Idea: Change the heading to *Set Sail with (Mr. B's) Second Grade!* Have students write on the scrolls five reasons why they like their class. Blue background ✤ Turkey border (CTP 0157)

Mayflower Messages

After studying the history of Thanksgiving, enlarge, trace, and cut out the *Mayflower* and attach it to the center of a bulletin board titled *Mayflower Messages.* Invite each student to pretend he or she is a passenger on the *Mayflower* and write a letter about his or her journey to the "New World." Have students copy their letters on large torn pieces of paper grocery bags and roll the ends of the paper like scrolls. Staple the scrolls around the ship.

 **MATERIALS**

✪ *Mayflower* (page 175)
✪ *paper grocery bags*

Another Idea: Change the heading to *We Love to Gobble!* Have students write in the speech bubbles food they like to gobble at a Thanksgiving dinner. Yellow background ♣ Turkey border (CTP 0157)

Let's Talk Turkey

Enlarge, trace, color, and cut out the Turkey and staple it to the center of a bulletin board titled *Let's Talk Turkey*. Add colorful construction-paper feathers to the turkey. Invite each student to pretend he or she is a turkey and write sentences that try to persuade diners not to eat him or her for Thanksgiving. Have students copy the sentences inside the "speech bubble" on a Let's Talk Turkey reproducible. Ask students to color the turkeys and hang them on the bulletin board.

 **MATERIALS**

✪ *Turkey (page 176)*

✪ *Let's Talk Turkey (page 177)*

✪ *colored construction paper*

This Thanksgiving We Won't Forget

Something for Each Letter of the Alphabet!

Another Idea: Change the subject of the board to a field trip, such as a trip to the zoo. Change the heading to *Alphabet Adventures!*
Orange background

This Thanksgiving . . .

Assign a letter of the alphabet to each student. Invite students to use a camera to photograph an object or person (whose name begins with their assigned letter) they are thankful for. (Sign out a disposable camera for students who do not have one at home.) Invite each student to glue four tongue depressors on his or her photograph to frame it. Ask students to write on the frame the name of the object or person. Then have students glue a corresponding bulletin board letter to the frame. Attach the photos, in alphabetical order, to a bulletin board. Add the heading *This Thanksgiving We Won't Forget Something for Each Letter of the Alphabet!*

 MATERIALS

- disposable camera/film
- tongue depressors
- bulletin-board letters

Another Idea: Have students draw family trees on paper. Post the papers on the tree.

Green background ✤ Maple Leaves border (CTP 0138)

Family Tree

Twist brown butcher paper to resemble a tree trunk and branches. Staple the "tree" to a bulletin board. Invite each student to tear a large leaf shape from green, yellow, orange, red, or brown construction paper. Ask students to bring in a family photo and tape it to the center of their leaf. Staple the leaves on the paper tree. Title the bulletin board *Family Tree*.

 **MATERIALS**

☼ brown butcher paper

☼ green, yellow, orange, red, or brown construction paper

☼ family photos brought from home

Another Idea: Invite students to write jokes on the ears of corn.

Green background ♣ Candy Corn border (CTP 0341)

"Corny" Kids!

Photograph each student as he or she makes a silly face. Cut several "ears of corn" from yellow construction paper. Tape the photos in the centers of ears of corn. Attach several real or paper cornstalks to a bulletin board. Staple each ear of corn to a stalk and add the heading *"Corny" Kids!*

 **MATERIALS**

✪ *camera/film*

✪ *yellow construction paper*

✪ *real or paper cornstalks*

Let's Have a "Ball" of Fun!

 Cut a snowman shape from white butcher paper and tape it to your door. Add paper facial features, a real hat, paper buttons, real twig "arms," and a fabric-scrap scarf. Write each student's name on a white paper circle (snowball) and tape the circles around the snowman. Tape a "speech bubble" above the snowman and write inside *Let's Have a "Ball" of Fun!*

MATERIALS

✪ white butcher paper
✪ colored construction paper
✪ hat
✪ twigs
✪ fabric scraps
✪ white paper circles

Another Idea: Change the title to *Welcome to Our Winter Wonderland!*

Run, Run, as Fast as You Can...

Another Idea: Change the heading to *Sweet Christmas Dreams*. Have students write Christmas wishes on the Gingerbread Men.

Yellow background ❧ Gingerbread border (CTP 0364)

Run, Run, as Fast as You Can . . .

Enlarge, trace, color, and cut out the Gingerbread Man and attach it to a bulletin board titled *Run, Run, as Fast as You Can. . . .* Read aloud and discuss *The Gingerbread Man*. Ask students to think of a safe place they would run if they were the Gingerbread Man. Have students write their ideas in the center of a Gingerbread Man pattern. Invite students to decorate their Gingerbread Man with art supplies, cut him out, and staple him to the bulletin board.

 **MATERIALS**

- ✪ Gingerbread Man (page 178)
- ✪ The Gingerbread Man *retold by Carol North*
- ✪ art supplies

Red background ❖ Reindeer border (CTP 0156)

"Deer" Me!

Invite each student to trace his or her shoe on a piece of tan construction paper and cut it out. Then ask students to trace each hand on a piece of brown construction paper and cut those out. Have students glue the handprints to the shoe print so they resemble a reindeer head and antlers. Invite students to decorate the heads with art supplies. Attach the heads to a bulletin board titled *"Deer" Me!*

 MATERIALS

✪ tan and brown construction paper

✪ art supplies

Another Idea: Change the heading to *Christmas around the World* and have students write on their doll a Christmas fact about a specific country. Black background ❖ Icicles border (CTP 0362) ❖ Blue/Yellow Star Cut-Outs (CTP 4896)

Winter Celebrations around the World

Attach a large blue butcher-paper oval to the center of a bulletin board to represent the earth; then add green butcher-paper "continents." Add the heading *Winter Celebrations around the World.* Invite each student to choose a different country and use a Paper Doll pattern and art supplies to decorate a doll that represents that country. Have students cut out their dolls and attach them to the bulletin board. Write on paper star cut-outs the names of several winter celebrations such as Christmas (a Christian holiday), Chanukah (a Jewish holiday), Kwanzaa (an African-American holiday), Divali (a Hindu holiday), Loy Krathong (a Thai holiday), and Ramadan (a Muslim holiday). Attach the stars to the bulletin board.

 **MATERIALS**

- ✪ large blue butcher-paper oval
- ✪ green butcher paper
- ✪ Paper Doll (page 179)
- ✪ art supplies
- ✪ paper star cut-outs

Another Idea: Change the heading to *We're Going "Ding Dong" for Onomatopoeias!* Have students write "sound words" on the bells. Green background ✤ Candy Canes border (CTP 0343)

Our Bells Are Ringing . . .

Have each student write on a Bell what would make his or her "bells ring" (in other words, what would make him or her happy) during the current holiday season. Invite students to color the bells and cut them out. Ask students to punch two holes near the top of the bells; string red, green, or gold ribbon through the holes; and tie a bow. Hang the bells on a bulletin board titled *Our Bells Are Ringing for a Happy Holiday Season!*

 **MATERIALS**

✪ Bells (page 180)

✪ red, green, or gold ribbon

May These Gifts Be Yours This Holiday Season and Always.

Red background ✤ Candy Canes border (CTP 0343)

May These Gifts . . .

Attach a green butcher-paper evergreen tree to the center of a bulletin board. Add the heading *May These Gifts Be Yours This Holiday Season and Always.* Invite each student to decorate a box top with wrapping paper and ribbons. Have each student think of a word that represents an intangible gift he or she could give someone, such as *love, joy, hope, comfort, respect, happiness, kindness,* or *trust.* Ask students to write their word on a large gift tag and tape the tag to the box top. Arrange the box tops under the paper tree so they look like gift boxes.

 **MATERIALS**

- ✪ green butcher-paper evergreen tree
- ✪ box tops
- ✪ wrapping paper
- ✪ ribbons
- ✪ large gift tags

Nine little candles,
Burning bright,
Tell of a temple
Full of light!

Blue background ❖ Ice Crystals border (CTP 0142)

Nine Little Candles, Burning Bright

Enlarge, trace, color, and cut out a Menorah and attach it to the center of a bulletin board. Add the following poem for a heading:

> Nine little candles,
> Burning bright,
> Tell of a temple
> Full of light!

Invite each student to think of a Chanukah wish for others and write it on a Star of David. Have students color their star, cut it out, and attach it to the bulletin board.

 **MATERIALS**

✪ Menorah (page 181)
✪ Star of David (page 182)

Another Idea: Change the heading to *Books Make Us Burst with Excitement!*

Gold background ✤ Balloons border (CTP 0203)

A Bunch of New Year's Resolutions!

Invite each student to cut two identical balloon shapes from construction paper. Have students place one shape on the other. Ask students to write on the top shape their resolution for the new year. Have students staple three-quarters of the way around the stacked shapes. Invite students to stuff the shapes with newspaper and staple them closed to create a 3-D balloon. Staple curling ribbon to the bottom of each balloon, staple the balloons in a bunch on the bulletin board, and gather and tie the curling ribbon near the bottom. Attach New Year's noisemakers, hats, and tiaras to the bulletin board. Add the heading *A Bunch of New Year's Resolutions!*

 **MATERIALS**

✪ construction paper
✪ newspaper
✪ curling ribbon
✪ New Year's noisemakers, hats, and tiaras

Another Idea: Change the title to *Make Magic with Science!* Write the names of science experiments on stars as you complete them as a class.
Gold background ✤ Gold Stars border (CTP 0151) ✤ Blue/Yellow Star Cut-Outs (CTP 4896)

Make (Year) a Magical Year!

Cut from black butcher paper a magician's hat and staple it upside down to the center of a bulletin board. Staple gold-foil or silver-foil stars "in" the hat and attach a black paper-covered ruler "magic wand" near the brim. Add the heading *Make (date of the new year) a Magical Year!* Invite each student to write on a paper star cut-out a New Year's resolution and his or her name. Hang the stars around the hat.

 **MATERIALS**

✪ black butcher paper
✪ gold-foil or silver-foil stars
✪ paper star cut-outs

Blue background ✤ Patriotic Decor border (CTP 0348)

He Had a Dream. I Have One Too!

Enlarge, trace, color, and cut out the Martin Luther King, Jr. reproducible and attach it to the center of a bulletin board. Ask students to draw on an index card a "dream" they have for peace in their school, neighborhood, country, or world. Then invite each student to glue stretched cotton balls onto a white paper cloud shape. Ask students to glue their index card on the cloud. Attach the clouds to a bulletin board titled *He Had a Dream. I Have One Too!*

 **MATERIALS**

✪ *Martin Luther King, Jr. (page 183)*

✪ *index cards*

✪ *cotton balls*

✪ *white paper cloud shapes*

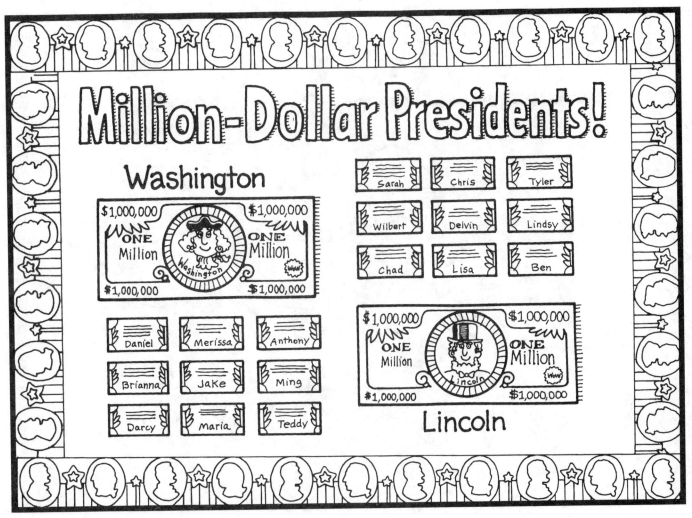

Blue background ❖ Presidents border (CTP 0357)

Million-Dollar Presidents!

Enlarge, trace, color, and cut out each "Million-Dollar President" Bill. Attach the bills to a bulletin board titled *Million-Dollar Presidents!* Invite each student to choose one of the presidents and write on a green construction-paper rectangle why that president was a "million-dollar" leader. Have students decorate their rectangle to look like money. Attach the rectangles to the bulletin board.

 **MATERIALS**

✪ "Million-Dollar President" Bills (page 184)

✪ green construction-paper rectangles

Another Idea: Have students write *I want (friend's name) to be my valentine because* _____ on the hearts.

Pink background ❧ Heart Cookies border (CTP 0345) ❧ Red/Pink Heart Cut-Outs (CTP 4891)

I'm Aiming for Your Heart, Valentine!

Enlarge, trace, color, and cut out the Cupid and staple it to the center of the bulletin board. Invite each student to use art supplies to decorate a paper heart cut-out. Have each student cut two diagonal slits through his or her heart and insert a drinking straw into the slits. Ask students to tape a small paper triangle to one end of the straw to make the straw into an "arrow." Then have students push clay into the other end of the straw and insert a feather into the clay. Have students staple their hearts to the bulletin board. Add the heading *I'm Aiming for Your Heart, Valentine!*

 **MATERIALS**

- ✪ Cupid (page 185)
- ✪ art supplies
- ✪ paper heart cut-outs
- ✪ drinking straws
- ✪ small paper triangles
- ✪ clay
- ✪ feathers

White and Blue background (see activity directions) ✤ Ski Caps border (CTP 0344)

Don't Let Your Work Go "Downhill"!

Staple a white butcher-paper "toboggan hill" to a blue background. Then invite each student to color and cut out a sled and "sledder" from the Sled reproducible. Ask students to write on the sled a sentence that gives advice about how to keep schoolwork from going "downhill," such as *Put your name on your paper* or *Check your work*. Attach the sleds and sledders to the bulletin board. Add the heading *Don't Let Your Work Go "Downhill"*!

 **MATERIALS**

- ○ white butcher paper
- ○ blue butcher paper
- ○ Sled (page 186)

Another Idea: Change words on the mittens to capital and lowercase letters, friends' names, or number symbols and names.

Yellow background ♣ Ski Caps border (CTP 0344) ♣ Blue/Pink Mitten Cut-Outs (CTP 4875)

Perfect Pairs

Invite each student to decorate with art supplies a pair of paper mitten cut-outs. Have each student think of two synonyms and write each synonym on a different mitten. Ask students to punch holes in the mitten tops and connect them with yarn. Hang the mittens on a bulletin board titled *Perfect Pairs*.

 **MATERIALS**

✪ art supplies

✪ paper mitten cut-outs

✪ hole punch

✪ yarn

Aluminum-foil background (see activity directions) ✤ Ice Crystals border (CTP 0142)

People Are like Snowflakes

Cover a bulletin board with an aluminum-foil background and add the heading *People Are like Snowflakes. Each One Is Unique.* Invite each student to make a white cut-paper snowflake and glue a photocopy of his or her photo in the center of the snowflake. Have students trace the snowflakes with glue and sprinkle glitter over the glue. Staple the snowflakes to the bulletin board.

 **MATERIALS**

✪ *aluminum foil*

✪ *white construction paper*

✪ *photocopies of student photos*

✪ *glitter*

✪ *glue*

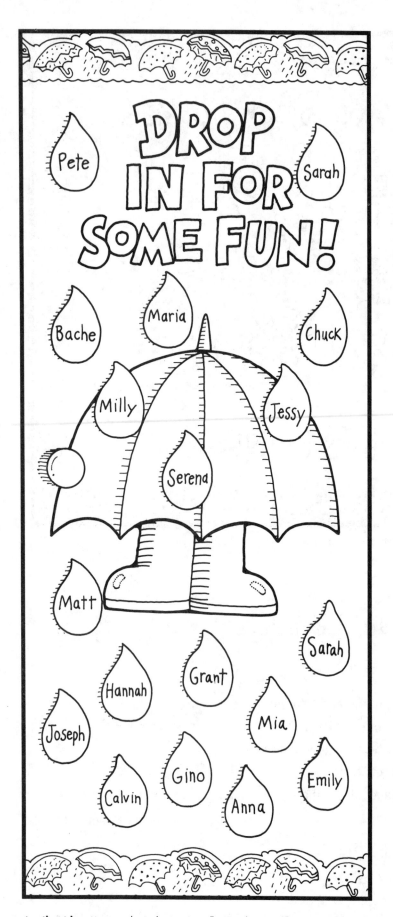

Drop In for Some Fun!

Cut a large umbrella shape from butcher paper and tape it to the classroom door. Tape two construction-paper rain boots under the umbrella. Write each student's name on a paper raindrop cut-out. Tape the cut-outs around and on the umbrella. Add the heading *Drop In for Some Fun!*

MATERIALS

- butcher paper
- construction paper
- paper raindrop cut-outs

Another Idea: Have each student write a "rainy-day word" on a raindrop. Change the heading to *It's Raining Rainy Words!*

Umbrellas border (CTP 0337) ✤ Dark Blue/Light Blue Raindrop Cut-Outs (CTP 4860)

Another Idea: Have students brainstorm and draw their own March similes. Change the heading to a student suggestion and post the drawings. Blue background ✤ Spring Blooms border (CTP 0338)

March Comes In like a Lion . . .

Enlarge, trace, color, and cut out the Lion and Lamb. Glue strands of yellow and gold yarn to the lion's mane and staple it to the left side of a bulletin board. Glue cotton balls on the lamb's body and staple the lamb to the right side of a bulletin board. Add the heading *March Comes In like a Lion and Goes Out like a Lamb!*

 **MATERIALS**

✪ *Lion (page 187)*
✪ *Lamb (page 188)*
✪ *yellow and gold yarn*
✪ *cotton balls*

Another Idea: Have students write on the pot a wish they would make if they caught a leprechaun.

Yellow background ♣ Shamrocks border (CTP 0118)

Lucky Leprechauns

Enlarge, trace, color, and cut out a Leprechaun and staple it to a bulletin board titled *Lucky Leprechauns*. Invite each student to color and cut out a leprechaun and write on its pot of gold one reason why he or she is lucky. Staple the leprechauns on the bulletin board.

 **MATERIALS**

✪ Leprechaun (page 189)

A Basket of Babies That Hatch from Eggs!

The eggs read:
- I live in a coop.
- I live under rocks.
- I live in the sand.
- I live in the water.
- I live in a pond.
- I live under logs.
- I live in the desert.
- I live in a swamp.
- I live on a farm.
- I live near the sea.
- I live in a nest.
- I live in a hole.
- I live in Australia.
- I live in the field.
- I live in a lake.

Green background ✤ Spring Bunnies border (CTP 0140) ✤ Orange/Pink Oval Cut-Outs (CTP 4851)

A Basket of Babies . . .

Cut out a large butcher-paper basket and staple it to a bulletin board. Twist butcher paper to make a basket handle and attach it to the basket. Cut a butcher-paper bow and add it to the handle. Ask each student to use two paper oval cut-outs as eggs. Have students staple the eggs together to make a book. Invite each student to think of an animal that hatches from an egg. Have students write on the "egg book" cover two clues to the animal's identity, such as *I live in a nest. I have a red breast. What am I?* Invite students to write the animal's name inside the book and add an illustration. Attach the eggs to the board so they appear to be in the basket. Add the heading *A Basket of Babies That Hatch from Eggs!*

 **MATERIALS**

❂ *butcher paper*
❂ *paper oval cut-outs*

Green background ❖ Spring Bunnies border (CTP 0140)

Baskets of Blessings

Enlarge, trace, color, and cut out the Bunny and staple it to the center of a bulletin board titled *Baskets of Blessings*. Invite each student to color and cut out a Basket and write his or her name on it. Then ask students to think of five things for which they are thankful and write each thing on an egg in the basket. Hang the baskets around the bunny.

 **MATERIALS**

✪ Bunny (page 190)

✪ Basket (page 191)

Another Idea: Change the heading to *We "Dig" Reading!* Have students write (with crayon) on the mounds of dirt one reason why they like reading. Black background ♣ Fragile Earth border (CTP 0252)

We "Dig" Earth Day!

Attach a large blue butcher-paper oval to the center of a bulletin board to represent the earth; then add green butcher-paper "continents." Staple the earth to the center of a bulletin board titled *We "Dig" Earth Day!* Invite each student to design a construction-paper shovel and write on the handle *I "dig" Earth Day because. . . .* Cut from sandpaper a "mound of dirt" for each student and glue the shovels to the mounds. Attach the shovels and mounds to the bulletin board.

 **MATERIALS**

☻ *blue and green butcher paper*

☻ *construction paper*

☻ *sandpaper*

Another Idea: Change the heading to *We Love Farm Animals*. Make the collage from animal pictures and have students draw farm animals.
White background ❖ Heart Cookies border (CTP 0345)

Mommy & Me!

Cut a large heart from red butcher paper and attach it to a bulletin board. Invite students to cut out "mother and child" magazine pictures and glue them to the heart to make a collage. Then ask students to illustrate on construction paper a picture of themselves and their mother (or a special female friend). Staple the pictures around the heart. Add the heading *Mommy & Me!*

 **MATERIALS**

✪ red butcher paper
✪ magazines
✪ construction paper

Come On In–We're Having a Ball!

Color and cut out a large butcher-paper circle to represent a beach ball. Write each student's name on the ball. Tape the ball to the door. Cut curved black construction-paper strips and tape them above and below the ball so the ball looks like it is bouncing. Add the heading *Come On In—We're Having a Ball!*

MATERIALS

⭐ butcher paper
⭐ construction paper

Another Idea: Change the heading to *We're Ready to Bounce Back from a Long Summer!*

Another Idea: Change the heading to *You Brighten My Day!* Invite students to write on a sun an affirmation or a positive message each day. Post the suns on the board.

Orange background ♣ Sunny Smiles border (CTP 0352) ♣ Yellow/Orange Sun Cut-Outs (CTP 4859)

"Sun"sational Work!

Cut a large sun from yellow butcher paper and staple it to the center of a bulletin board. Add the heading *"Sun"sational Work!* Write each student's name on a paper sun cut-out. Choose a good-work sample for each student and tape his or her sun to the top left corner of the paper. Staple the good-work samples around the large sun.

 **MATERIALS**

✪ *yellow butcher paper*

✪ *paper sun cut-outs*

✪ *good-work samples*

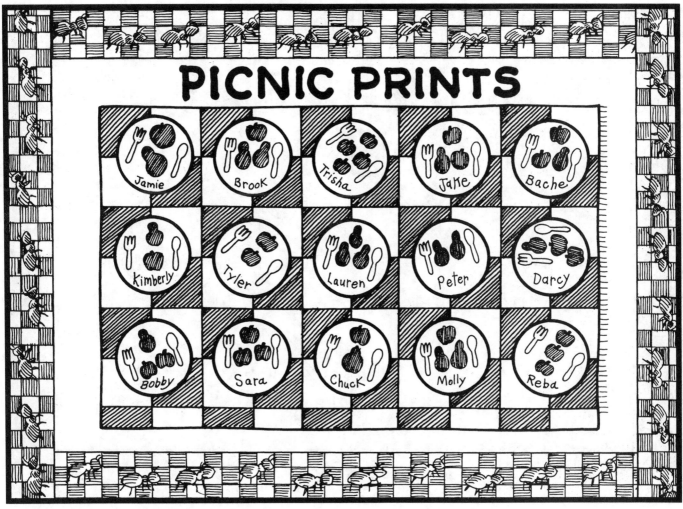

PICNIC PRINTS

Plates labeled: Jamie, Brook, Trisha, Jake, Bache, Kimberly, Tyler, Lauren, Peter, Darcy, Bobby, Sara, Chuck, Molly, Reba

Green background ♣ Picnic Ants border (CTP 0330)

Picnic Prints

Staple a red checkered tablecloth to a bulletin board. Invite each student to dip apple and pear halves in tempera paint and stamp them on a paper plate. When the paint is dry, have students glue a plastic fork and spoon to the plate. Hang the plates on the tablecloth and add the heading *Picnic Prints*.

 **MATERIALS**

✪ *red checkered tablecloth*

✪ *apple and pear halves*

✪ *tempera paint*

✪ *paper plates*

✪ *plastic forks and spoons*

Home Run Spellers!

Another Idea: Change the heading to *Home Run Hitters!* Use one ball for each student team and advance the teams around the bases as they show good behavior.

Green background ✤ Sports border (CTP 0356)

Home Run Spellers!

Staple thick yarn to a bulletin board to form a "baseball diamond." Add the heading *Home Run Spellers!* Cut out a white construction-paper circle (baseball) for each student, draw red "stitches" on each ball, and write the student's name on it. Set a spelling-test goal for each student, such as two or less incorrect words on a test, and challenge students to make the goal for four weeks. When students make their goal after the first week, place their baseball next to "first base" on the bulletin board. Advance the baseballs around the bases until students reach their goal four times.

 MATERIALS

✪ *thick yarn*

✪ *white construction-paper circles*

Another Idea: Change the heading to *Rollerblading Rules*. Invite each student to write on a rollerblade a rollerblading safety tip.
Black background ✤ Sports border (CTP 0356)

We're Ready to Roll with Subtraction!

Invite each student to choose a number and think of a subtraction equation that equals it. Have students write the equation (without the answer) on a Rollerblade. Have students color and cut out the rollerblade, fold down the tongue and write the answer to their equation on the inside. Invite students to punch holes in the "shoelace holes," thread a piece of yarn through the holes in the rollerblade, and tie the yarn into a bow. Attach the rollerblades to a bulletin board titled *We're Ready to Roll with Subtraction!* Invite students to visit the board, mentally solve the equations, and fold up the rollerblade tongues to check their answers.

 **MATERIALS**

✪ Rollerblade (page 192)
✪ hole punch
✪ yarn

A SLICE OF COUNTING FUN

Another Idea: Change the heading to *Juicy Stories*. Staple students' stories near each slice.

Green background ♣ Watermelons border (CTP 0347)

A Slice of Counting Fun

Cut a large slice of watermelon from pink and green butcher paper and staple it to the center of a bulletin board titled *A Slice of Counting Fun*. Cut black construction-paper "seeds" and add them to the slice. Invite each student to glue green tissue-paper squares on the rim of a paper-plate half and cover the rest of the plate half with pink tissue-paper squares. Have students glue several real watermelon seeds to their slice and use permanent marker to record on a plastic knife the number of seeds. Attach the watermelon slices and knives to the bulletin board.

 **MATERIALS**

- ✪ pink and green butcher paper
- ✪ black construction paper
- ✪ pink and green tissue-paper squares
- ✪ paper-plate halves
- ✪ real watermelon seeds
- ✪ permanent markers
- ✪ plastic knives

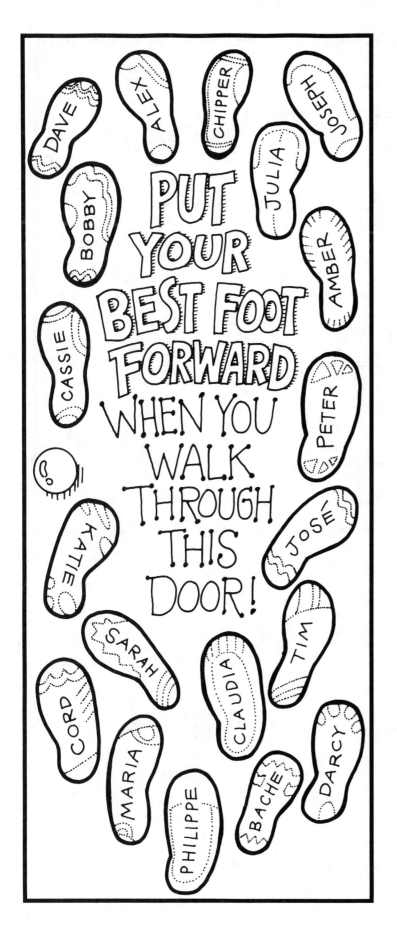

Put Your Best Foot Forward . . .

 Invite each student to bring in an old shoe, paint the shoe bottom with tempera paint, and make a stamped footprint on construction paper. Have students cut out the footprint and write their name on it. Tape the footprints to the classroom door under the heading *Put Your Best Foot Forward When You Walk through This Door!*

MATERIALS

✪ old shoes brought by students
✪ tempera paint/paintbrushes
✪ construction paper

Black background ❖ Sunny Smiles border (CTP 0352)

Share a Smile—It's Worth Your While!

Invite each student to paint a paper plate yellow. When the plates are dry, ask each student to paint a black smiley face on the plate. Attach the plates to a bulletin board titled *Share a Smile—It's Worth Your While!*

 **MATERIALS**

✪ paper plates
✪ yellow and black tempera paint/paintbrushes

Another Idea: Change the heading to *Be a Good "Neigh"-bor!* Invite students to draw illustrations of themselves being neighborly in and out of the classroom.

Green background ❖ Picket Fence border (CTP 0358)

No Horsin' Around!

Enlarge, trace, color, and cut out the Horse and attach it to the center of a bulletin board titled *No Horsin' Around!* Invite each student to draw on construction paper an illustration of himself or herself following a classroom rule or procedure. Attach the illustrations to the bulletin board.

 **MATERIALS**

✪ Horse (page 193)

✪ white construction paper

Another Idea: Change the heading to *Un"bee"lievable Work!* Post student work near the bees.

Floral Wrapping Paper background (see activity directions) ♣ Photo Frame Busy Bees border (CTP 0327)

Be a Busy Bee!

Cover a bulletin board with floral wrapping paper and add the heading *Be a Busy Bee!* Invite each student to color and cut out a Bee. Have each student cut an hourglass shape from waxed paper, draw intersecting lines on the waxed paper with black permanent marker, and gather the paper in the center with a twist tie to form "bee wings." Have students tape the wings to their bee. Staple the bees to the bulletin board. Write on sentence strips a "be phrase" for each bee, such as *Be Kind! Be Helpful!* or *Be a Good Listener!* Staple a sentence strip under each bee.

 **MATERIALS**

✪ *floral wrapping paper*
✪ *Bee (page 194)*
✪ *waxed paper*
✪ *black permanent markers*
✪ *twist ties*
✪ *sentence strips*

Another Idea: Change the title to *Give the Gift of Friendship!* Have students wrap the boxes with butcher paper and decorate the paper with sentences that describe how they can be a friend to others.

Blue background ❖ Rainbow Pencils border (CTP 0256)

Give the Gift of Respect!

Use colorful wrapping paper and ribbons to wrap seven boxes. Write each letter of the word *respect* on a different box. Place double-sided tape on the box bottoms and arrange the boxes in order on a bulletin board titled *Give the Gift of Respect!*

 **MATERIALS**

✪ *colorful wrapping paper*
✪ *ribbons*
✪ *seven boxes*
✪ *double-sided tape*

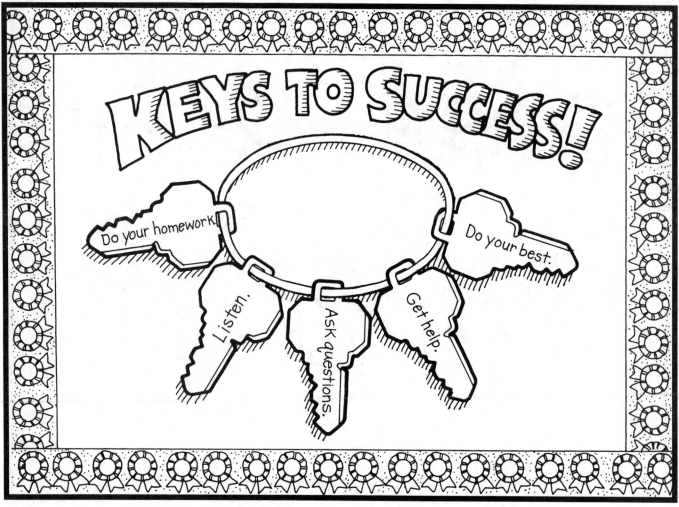

Another Idea: Make the heading specific, such as *Keys to Success in Math!* Write "success tips" for the subject on the keys.

Purple background ✤ Rainbow Ribbons border (CTP 0353)

Keys to Success!

Reproduce several Keys on tagboard and cut them out. Cover the keys with aluminum foil, punch holes in the tops, and string them onto thick yarn. Use permanent marker to write on each key a phrase about positive behavior that leads to success in school. Staple the keys to a bulletin board titled *Keys to Success!*

 **MATERIALS**

- ✪ Key (page 195)
- ✪ tagboard
- ✪ aluminum foil
- ✪ thick yarn
- ✪ permanent marker

I Look In the Mirror and What Do I See? Someone Very Special— I See Me!

Another Idea: Change the heading to *Mirror, Mirror, on the Wall . . . Who's the Fairest of Them All?* Invite students to design either a paper-plate "evil queen" face or a paper-plate Snow White face. Post the faces around the mirror.

Gold background ✤ Kids of the World border (CTP 0143)

I Look In the Mirror . . .

Attach a mirror to a bulletin board so students can see their faces when they stand in front of the board. Invite each student to use a paper plate and art supplies to design a face that represents himself or herself. Hang the paper-plate faces around the mirror and add the heading *I Look In the Mirror and What Do I See? Someone Very Special—I See Me!*

 **MATERIALS**

✪ mirror with a wire on the back

✪ paper plates

✪ art supplies

Light Blue background ♣ Clouds and Kites border (CTP 0346)

All Ideas Start as Dreams . . .

Invite each student to cut a cloud shape from white construction paper. Have students write in the center of the cloud one dream they have for the future. Instruct students to stretch and glue cotton balls around the edge of the cloud. Staple the clouds to a light-blue bulletin board background. Add the heading *All Ideas Start as Dreams—Big, Small, and In Between!*

 **MATERIALS**

✪ white construction paper

✪ cotton balls

✪ light-blue butcher paper

Light Blue background ✤ Read a Book border (CTP 0134)

Manners Matter!

Enlarge, trace, color, and cut out Miss Manners and staple her to the center of a bulletin board titled *Manners Matter!* Invite each student to fold a piece of white construction paper to make a book and write *Miss Manner's Book of Etiquette* on the cover. Have students write and illustrate a "manners rule" inside the book. Staple the books to the bulletin board.

 MATERIALS

✪ *Miss Manners (page 196)*

✪ *white construction paper*

Green background ♣ Sports border (CTP 0356)

Your Work Is Really "on the Ball"!

Draw red lines on a large white butcher-paper circle so it resembles a baseball. Staple the "baseball" to a bulletin board and add the heading *Your Work Is Really "on the Ball"!* Each time students perform well on an assignment, invite them to write their name on a white construction-paper circle and staple it next to the good-work sample on the bulletin board. When students have attached three work samples to the board, present them with a small treat.

 **MATERIALS**

✪ *large white butcher-paper circle*

✪ *white construction-paper circles*

✪ *good-work samples*

✪ *small treats*

Another Idea: *Make the heading subject specific, such as I Shine at Spelling. Add a sun ray each time a student performs well in that subject.*

Orange background ❖ Sunny Smiles border (CTP 0352)

I Can Shine!

Draw a happy face on a large yellow butcher-paper circle to make a sun. Staple the sun to the center of a bulletin board titled *I Can Shine!* Write each student's name on a yellow paper strip "sun ray." Tell students that you will place their sun ray on the sun when you observe them following a classroom rule or setting a good example for others. Staple the sun rays to the sun until each student's ray is on the bulletin board. Then reward the class with a "sunny treat."

 **MATERIALS**

❂ *yellow butcher-paper circle*

❂ *yellow paper strips*

❂ *"sunny treats" (sunflower seeds, orange juice, etc.)*

Another Idea: Change the heading to *"Tree"mendous Job!* Post student work on the tree.

Green background ✤ Spring Blooms border (CTP 0338) ✤ Red/Yellow Maple Leaf Cut-Outs (CTP 4900) ✤ Red/Yellow Flower Cut-Outs (CTP 4897)

Good Deeds like These Don't Grow on Trees!

Twist brown butcher paper to form a tree trunk and branches and attach it to a bulletin board titled *Good Deeds like These Don't Grow on Trees!* Each time a student performs a good deed or a "random act of kindness," write his or her name and the good deed on a paper leaf or flower cut-out and attach it to the tree.

 **MATERIALS**

- ⊙ brown butcher paper
- ⊙ paper leaf and flower cut-outs

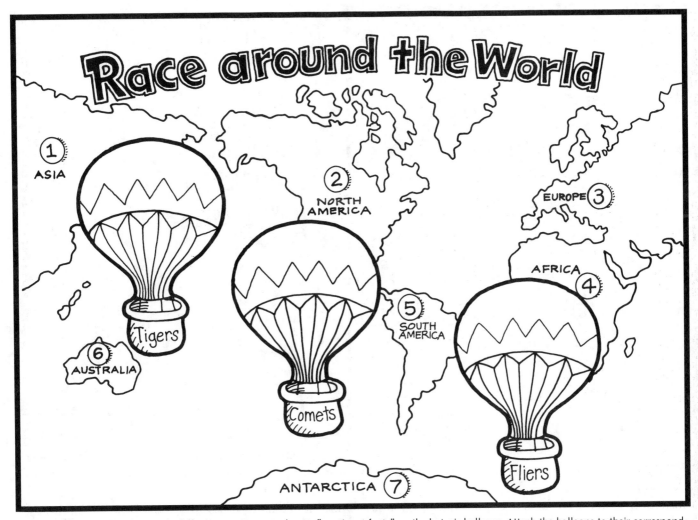

Another Idea: Have the class study different continents and write "continent facts" on the hot-air balloons. Attach the balloons to their corresponding continents. Change the heading to *Around the World in (number of days in the unit) Days!*

Blue background

Race around the World

Staple a large world map to the center of a bulletin board titled *Race around the World*. Write a different number (from one to seven) on each of the continents. Divide the class into groups. Have each group color and cut out a Balloon and then write their group name on the balloon basket. Tack all the balloons on Continent I. Explain that you will move each balloon from continent to continent as you observe students in that group showing good behavior. Tell students that the first group to reach Continent 7 will be the winner. Move the balloons until one group reaches Continent 7. Then provide the winners with a treat such as extra library or computer time.

 **MATERIALS**

✪ *large world map*

✪ *Balloon (page 197)*

A Roomful of Bright Ideas!

 Cut a large lightbulb from white butcher paper and tape it to your classroom door. Draw details on the lightbulb and write *A Roomful of Bright Ideas!* in the center. Choose a good-work sample for each student and overlap and tape the samples around the perimeter of the lightbulb as an outline.

MATERIALS

✪ white butcher paper
✪ good-work samples

Another Idea: Change the heading to *"Cow" Makes the "ow" Sound!* Invite students to write on index cards other words that have the "ow" sound. Post the cards on the described frames.

Green background

"Moo"velous Job!

Enlarge, trace, color, and cut out the Cow and staple it to the center of a bulletin board. Add the heading *"Moo"velous Job!* Invite each student to staple a good-work sample to a piece of black construction paper. Ask students to use white crayon to color "cow spots" around the edges of the black paper to create a frame. Staple the work samples around the cow.

 **MATERIALS**

- ✪ Cow (page 198)
- ✪ black construction paper
- ✪ good-work samples
- ✪ white crayon

Your Work Is Right on Track!

Miguel Brandi Neil

Bobbie Jeff Vicki Everett

Bradly Chrissy Colleen Tommy

Blaire Renee Nita Cal

Blue background ✤ Wow! border (CTP 0155)

Your Work Is Right on Track!

Enlarge, trace, color, and cut out one engine and several rail cars (one rail car per student). Write a student's name on each rail car. Attach the engine and the sides and bottoms of the rail cars to a bulletin board titled *Your Work Is Right on Track!* Each week, choose a good-work sample for each student and place it inside his or her rail car.

 **MATERIALS**

✪ Train (page 166)

✪ good-work samples

Another Idea: Change the heading to *Alphabet Soup*. Invite students to place in their bowl letter sounds they have mastered.

Gold background ✤ Super! border (CTP 0153)

"Soup"er Work!

Invite each student to decorate and cut out a large "soup bowl" from construction paper. Have students glue a plastic spoon to the outside of the bowl and write their name on the spoon. Staple the sides and bottoms of the bowls to a bulletin board so they become pockets. Label the board *"Soup"er Work!* Each week, invite each student to choose a good-work sample and place it inside his or her soup bowl.

 **MATERIALS**

✪ construction paper

✪ plastic spoons

✪ good-work samples

Another Idea: Change the heading to *We Hatch Some Great Ideas!* Post science journal entries near the eggs.

Purple background ✤ Rainbow Ribbons border (CTP 0353)

"Egg"cellent Students!

Invite each student to draw on construction paper a small self-portrait that shows the body from the waist up. Have students cut out their portraits and place them inside a half of a plastic egg. Write each student's name on his or her egg. Use double-sided tape to attach each egg half to a bulletin board titled *"Egg"cellent Students!* Staple a good-work sample for each student next to each corresponding egg.

 **MATERIALS**

- ✪ construction paper
- ✪ plastic eggs
- ✪ double-sided tape
- ✪ good-work samples

Another Idea: Change the heading to *We're Fired Up about Reading!* Post book reports near student firecrackers.

Red background ✤ Patriotic Decor border (CTP 0348)

You Did a Bang-Up Job!

Invite each student to color a small cardboard tube with red, white, and blue crayons. Ask each student to write his or her name on the decorated tube. Have each student tape red, white, and blue paper strips and tinsel or curling ribbon to one end of the tube to make a "firecracker." Display a good-work sample for each student on a bulletin board. Have students staple their firecracker next to their work. Add the heading *You Did a Bang-Up Job!*

 **MATERIALS**

- ✪ small cardboard tubes
- ✪ red, white, and blue crayons
- ✪ red, white, and blue paper strips
- ✪ tinsel or curling ribbon
- ✪ good-work samples

Another Idea: Change the heading to *Let's Have a Banner Day!* Invite students to write on their banner one thing they can do to have a banner day. Blue background

Banner Ideas!

Cut a long strip from a bedsheet to make a banner that spans the length of a bulletin board. Use fabric paint on the strip to paint the words *Banner Ideas!* Hang the sheet across the top of the bulletin board. Cut small "banners" from the rest of the sheet, one banner for each student. Invite students to decorate a small banner with their name. Hang the banners on the bulletin board. Invite students to choose a good-work sample and staple it under their banner.

 **MATERIALS**

✪ bedsheet

✪ fabric paint

✪ good-work samples

Another Idea: Change the heading to *Get Some School "Spirit"!* Have students surround the ghost with written or drawn ideas for school unity and enthusiasm.

Purple background ❖ Black/Purple Halloween Bat Cut-Outs used as border (CTP 4872)

"Boo"tiful Job!

Gather a large section of bedsheet in the center and staple it to a bulletin board to resemble a ghost. Draw eyes and a smile on the ghost. Attach a good-work sample for each student around the ghost. Add the heading *"Boo"tiful Job!*

 **MATERIALS**

✪ bedsheet
✪ good-work samples

Another Idea: Change the heading to *We're Quacking about "Qu"!* Have students insert in their duck a card with a "qu" word.
Blue background

Your Work Is "Just Ducky"!

Invite each student to color and cut out a Duck. Have students cover their ducks with yellow craft feathers. Staple the sides and bottom of the ducks to a bulletin board titled *Your Work Is "Just Ducky"!* Write each student's name near his or her duck. Each week, insert a good-work sample for each student into the pocket made by each duck.

 **MATERIALS**

✪ Duck (page 199)

✪ yellow craft feathers

✪ good-work samples

Another Idea: Change the heading to *If I Only Had a Brain.* . . . Invite students to write a letter to the scarecrow and tell him how he can become more intelligent. Post the letters on the board.

Gold background ✤ Pumpkins border (CTP 0139)

Your Work Is Something to Crow About!

Use scarecrow supplies (see materials list) to make a scarecrow and staple it to the center of a bulletin board titled *Your Work Is Something to Crow About!* Then reproduce on black paper a Crow for each student and cut out the crows. Write a student's name on each crow with chalk or white crayon, attach each crow to a good-work sample, and staple the samples to the bulletin board.

 **MATERIALS**

✪ *scarecrow supplies (burlap, children's clothing, straw hat, straw, construction paper, rope)*

✪ *black construction paper*

✪ *Crow (page 200)*

✪ *chalk or white crayon*

✪ *good-work samples*

Another Idea: Have students write fairy tales with a dragon as the main character. Attach the stories to the board and change the heading to *These Dragon Stories Are So Hot, They're Breathing Fire!*

Black background

These Grades Are "Hot"!

Enlarge, trace, color, and cut out the Dragon and attach it to the center of a bulletin board titled *These Grades Are "Hot"!* Attach red and orange metallic paper strips to the board so they look like fire coming out of the dragon's mouth. Surround the dragon with a good-work sample for each student.

MATERIALS

✪ *Dragon (page 201)*

✪ *red and orange metallic paper strips (gift bag stuffing)*

✪ *good-work samples*

Another Idea: Surround the moon with popular "moon words" and phrases, such as *moonlighting, the man & the moon,* or *moonstruck*. Change the heading to *Moon Words*.

Blue background ❖ Gold Stars border (CTP 0151) ❖ Blue/Yellow Star Cut-Outs (CTP 4896)

My Stars! You're Bright!

Cut out a large quarter moon from poster board and cover it with aluminum foil. Add facial features and attach the face to the center of a bulletin board titled *My Stars! You're Bright!* Write a student's name on each star cut-out. Attach each star to a good-work sample and attach the samples to the bulletin board.

 **MATERIALS**

☆ poster board

☆ aluminum foil

☆ paper star cut-outs

☆ good-work samples

Come On In and You Will See, Reading Is as Easy as ABC!

Amber Zach Will Charles Laura Xavier Quincy Rob Hailey Fran Sadie Ed Kurt May Gil Oliver José Nett Isaac Don Taneisha Patsy Ungavo Vince Yolanda DD Bobby

Come On In . . .

Write each student's name on the bulletin board letter that corresponds to the first letter of his or her name. Tape the letters to the classroom door and add the heading *Come On In and You Will See, Reading Is as Easy as ABC!*

MATERIALS

✪ *bulletin board letters*

Another Idea: Change the heading to *Nifty Names*.

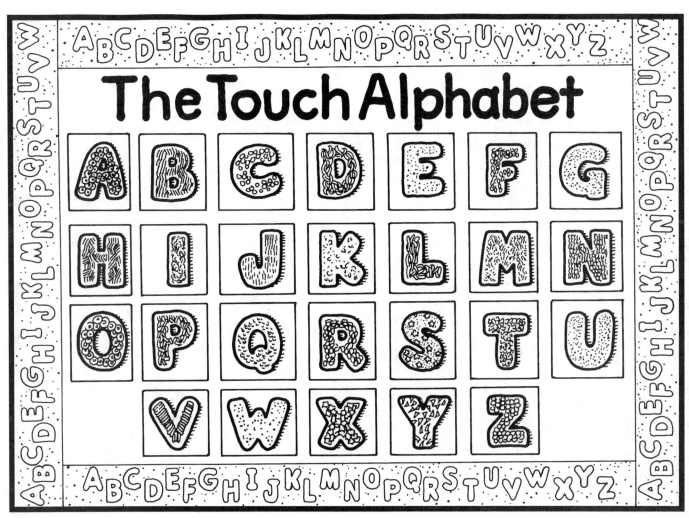

Orange background ♣ Alphabet Letters border (CTP 0350)

The Touch Alphabet

Invite each student to glue a different bulletin board letter (from *A* to *Z*) to the center of a piece of construction paper. Have students spread glue over the letter and sprinkle or place on top a small item whose name begins with that letter (such as Apple Jacks cereal for *A*, buttons for *B*, and cornmeal for *C*). Staple each letter to a bulletin board titled *The Touch Alphabet*. Invite students to visit the bulletin board and trace the letters with their fingers.

 MATERIALS

✪ bulletin board letters

✪ construction paper

✪ small items whose names begin with each letter of the alphabet

Another Idea: Change the heading to *We're Nuts for Letters!*

Hot Pink background ✤ Alphabet Letters border (CTP 0350)

Chicka Chicka Boom Boom . . .

Twist brown butcher paper to resemble the trunk of a palm tree and staple the trunk to a bulletin board titled *Chicka Chicka Boom Boom, These Are the Letters We Know in Our Room.* . . . Cut green butcher-paper palm fronds and attach them to the trunk. Cut 26 "coconuts" from brown construction paper and write on each coconut a letter of the alphabet. Read aloud *Chicka Chicka Boom Boom.* Explain that you will add coconuts to the tree throughout the year as the class learns letters. Attach a coconut each time a new letter is introduced until the tree is full.

 **MATERIALS**

✪ *brown and green butcher paper*

✪ *brown construction paper*

✪ Chicka Chicka Boom Boom *by Bill Martin, Jr. and John Archambault*

Yellow background ❧ Garden Creatures border (CTP 0145)

There Was an Old Lady . . .

Enlarge, trace, color, and cut out the Old Lady. Cut out the circle in her stomach and replace it with plastic wrap taped to the back side of the paper. Cut out a hole for the Old Lady's mouth. Attach the Old Lady to the center of a bulletin board titled *There Was an Old Lady. . . .* Color and cut out the Animals She Swallowed and tack them around the bulletin board. Invite students to visit the board, sing the song that corresponds to the board, and "feed" each animal to the Old Lady as students come to that part in the song. (If the bulletin board will not be interactive, place the animals in her stomach before stapling the images to the bulletin board.)

 **MATERIALS**

✪ *Old Lady (page 202)*

✪ *plastic wrap*

✪ *Animals She Swallowed (pages 203 and 204)*

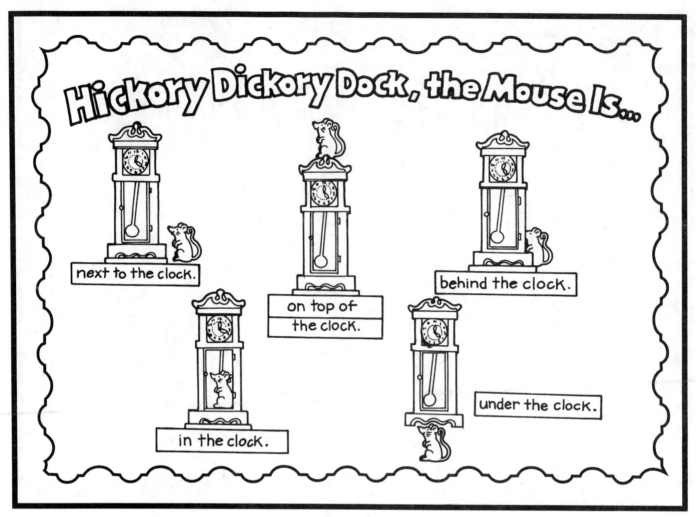

Gold background

Hickory Dickory Dock . . .

Write the words *next to the clock, under the clock, on top of the clock, in the clock,* and *behind the clock* on individual sentence strips and staple them to a bulletin board titled *Hickory Dickory Dock, the Mouse Is. . . .* Reproduce, color, and cut out five Mouse and Clock reproducibles. Staple each clock near a sentence strip and place each mouse on the clock that corresponds to the words on the strip.

 **MATERIALS**

✪ *sentence strips*

✪ *Mouse and Clock (page 205)*

Light Blue background ✤ Photo Frame Busy Bees border (CTP 0327)

We're Buzzing About . . .

Invite each student to draw on white construction paper an illustration of a favorite scene from a current read-aloud. Have students color and cut out a Bee and attach it to their illustration. Staple the illustrations to a bulletin board titled *We're Buzzing About (Book Title)*.

 **MATERIALS**

✪ *white construction paper*

✪ *read-aloud book*

✪ *Bee (page 194)*

Welcome to the Land of Literature!

Science Fiction Historical Fiction Poetry Realistic Fiction Folktale

Informational Book Biography

Picture Book

Gold background ✤ Read a Book border (CTP 0134)

Welcome to the Land of Literature!

Enlarge, trace, color, and cut out the Castle. Staple the castle to a bulletin board titled *Welcome to the Land of Literature!* Color and cut out the Princess and tack it next to the castle. Before beginning a read-aloud book, discuss as a class the book's genre. Attach the princess to the castle in the corresponding place. Move the princess as the class enjoys read-alouds throughout the year.

 **MATERIALS**

✪ *Castle and Princess (page 206)*
✪ *read-aloud book*

Another Idea: Have each student decorate a fish and draw a construction-paper book cover for a favorite book. Connect each fish and book cover with a string and hang all the fish under the original heading.

Light Blue background ♣ Seashells border (CTP 0349)

Get "Hooked" on Reading!

Display two or three books on a bookshelf or table under a bulletin board titled *Get "Hooked" on Reading!* Enlarge, trace, color, and cut out a Fish and attach it to the bulletin board. Cut out a construction-paper fin and tape it on the fish so it extends outward, perpendicular to the board. Tape a chopstick "fishing pole" to the fin and tape a long string to the end of the pole. Tape a construction-paper "fishing hook" to the end of the string and tape the hook to a book on the bookshelf or table.

 **MATERIALS**

- ✪ two or three books
- ✪ bookshelf or table
- ✪ Fish (page 167)
- ✪ construction paper
- ✪ chopstick
- ✪ string

Another Idea: Change the heading to *Reptiles Are Radical!* Have students write reptile facts on an Iguana reproducible. Post the iguanas on the board. Purple background ❧ Read a Book border (CTP 0134)

Leaping Lizards!

Enlarge, trace, color, and cut out the Iguana. Staple the Iguana to the center of a bulletin board and add the heading *Leaping Lizards! "I-gwanna" Read These Books—How about You?* Display several favorite classroom or library book jackets around the iguana.

 **MATERIALS**

✪ Iguana (page 207)

✪ classroom or library book jackets

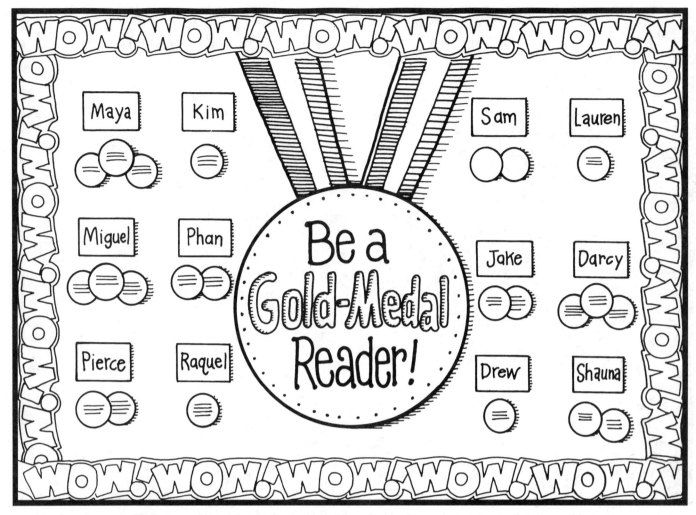

Another Idea: Change the heading to *Gold-Medal Multipliers!* Add medals to the board as students memorize their times tables.

Blue background ✤ Wow! border (CTP 0155)

Be a Gold-Medal Reader!

Punch a hole in the top of a large gold butcher-paper circle and string a piece of red, white, and blue ribbon through the hole. Hang the "gold medal" in the center of a bulletin board. Write *Be a Gold-Medal Reader!* in the center of the circle. Write a student's name on each slip of paper and attach each slip to the board. Place tacks under each name. Cut a small gold, gray, and brown construction-paper circle for each student to represent bronze, silver, and gold medals. Invite each student to read three books. When students finish the first book, have them write the book title on a brown circle and tack it under their name on the board. When students finish the second book, have them write the title on the gray circle and add it to the board. Have students add the gold circle when they finish the third book.

 **MATERIALS**

- ✪ hole punch
- ✪ gold butcher-paper circle
- ✪ red, white, and blue ribbon
- ✪ slips of paper
- ✪ gold, gray, and brown construction-paper circles

Purple background ♣ Grass border (CTP 0359)

A Basket of Beautiful Books

Staple the bottom and sides of a large tan butcher-paper basket to a bulletin board so it is a large "pocket." Twist a long strip of tan butcher paper to make a basket handle and attach it. Then, cut a butcher-paper bow and add it to the handle. Fill the basket with book jackets from Caldecott Medal Books and add the heading *A Basket of Beautiful Books.*

 **MATERIALS**

✪ large tan butcher-paper basket

✪ book jackets from Caldecott Medal Books

Another Idea: Change the heading to *You've Got the Cutest Little Baby Face!* Have students post their baby photos on the board.

Light Blue background

What Do You Say . . .

Enlarge, trace, color, and cut out the Baby and staple it to the center of a bulletin board titled *What Do You Say When You See a Cute Baby? "Aw!" "Au!"* Invite each student to think of an *aw* or *au* word and write it on an index card. Staple the cards to the bulletin board.

 **MATERIALS**

✪ Baby (page 208)

✪ index cards

Black background ✤ Rainbow Pencils border (CTP 0256)

A Rainbow of Many Colors

Make a quarter-circle butcher-paper rainbow and staple it to a bulletin board. Attach a white butcher-paper cloud to the top of the rainbow and write *A Rainbow of Many Colors* across the board. Attach a clean, empty can below each rainbow "stripe" to represent paint cans. Use permanent marker to write the name of each color in the rainbow on the handle of a different paintbrush and on each paint can. Place the paintbrushes in a container next to the board. Invite students to visit the board and place each paintbrush in the correct paint can.

 **MATERIALS**

- ✪ butcher paper (rainbow colors)
- ✪ white butcher paper
- ✪ clean, empty cans
- ✪ permanent markers
- ✪ paintbrushes

Another Idea: Change the heading to *Magnetic Personalities!* Invite student pairs to write about each other on a paper magnet before hanging.
Blue background

Opposites Attract!

Cut two large "horseshoe magnets" from red and gray butcher paper and staple the magnets to a bulletin board titled *Opposites Attract!* Write *North* on the left magnet and *South* on the right magnet. Draw "attraction lines" between the magnets. Have each student make two small horseshoe magnets from red and gray construction paper. Invite each student to think of a pair of antonyms and write each word on a magnet. Staple the magnet pairs to the bulletin board.

 **MATERIALS**

✪ red and gray butcher paper

✪ red and gray construction paper

Another Idea: Change the heading to *Fun with Frogs!* Invite students to write frog facts on a frog cut-out and staple their frog to a lily pad. Brown and Blue background (see activity directions) ❧ Light Green/Dark Green Frog Cut-Outs (CTP 4858)

Hoppin' Homonyms!

Write a different homonym on each of several paper frog cut-outs. Cut several lily pads from green construction paper and write the match to each homonym on a lily pad. Cover the bottom half of a bulletin board with brown butcher paper to represent the shore. Cover the top half with blue paper to represent the water. Staple the lily pads in the water and tack the frogs on the shore. Add the heading *Hoppin' Homonyms!* Invite students to visit the board and match each frog with the correct lily pad. Provide an answer key so students can correct their work.

 **MATERIALS**

✪ *paper frog cut-outs*

✪ *green construction paper*

✪ *brown and blue butcher paper*

✪ *answer key*

Riding the Rhyme Time Express

cat	sat	bat	rat	pat
in	pin	win	tin	bin
hop	top	stop	pop	crop
pan	ran	Stan	tan	can

Blue background

Riding the Rhyme Time Express

Reproduce and cut out four engines and sixteen rail cars from the Train reproducible. Color each engine and four cars one color to make four "train sets." Write an easy-to-rhyme word on each engine and staple the engines vertically to the left side of a bulletin board titled *Riding the Rhyme Time Express*. Write four words that rhyme with each engine word on each of the corresponding rail cars. Tack the rail cars horizontally, in random order, behind the engines. Invite students to come to the board, tack rail cars behind the correct engine, and silently read each word.

 **MATERIALS**

✪ *Train (page 166)*

Another Idea: Change the heading to *"Squ" Is Something to SQUeal About!* Invite students to write "squ" words on a Pig reproducible before hanging. Green background

What Rhymes with "Pig"?

Cut a large pig face from pink butcher paper and decorate it as shown. Staple the face to the center of a bulletin board and add the heading *What Rhymes with "Pig"?* Invite each student to color and cut out a pig from the Pig reproducible and write a rhyming word in the center. Staple the pigs around the pig face.

 **MATERIALS**

✪ *pink butcher paper*
✪ *Pig (page 209)*

Similes Are the "Write" Stuff!

Invite each student to color, cut out, and write his or her name on a Pencil. Ask students to write on the pencil a simile using the word *pencil*, such as *Her finger pointed at me like a sharp pencil.* Attach the pencils to the classroom door. Add the title *Similes Are the "Write" Stuff!*

 **MATERIALS**

✪ *Pencil (page 210)*

Another Idea: Change the heading to *"Write" On!* and hang student writing near each pencil.

Pencils border (CTP 0340)

Another Idea: Change the heading to *Look What's Cookin' in Math!* Write on the ingredient boxes explanations for current math concepts. Gold background ✤ Pencils border (CTP 0340)

We're Cookin' with the Writing Process!

Cut from black butcher paper a large cooking pot. Staple orange and yellow construction-paper flames to the bottom of a bulletin board and attach the pot over the flames. Cover five empty food containers with white construction paper and write one of the following words on each container: *Prewrite, Rough Draft, Edit, Final Draft, Publish*. Staple the containers to the bulletin board so they look like their contents are being poured into the pot. Draw "pouring lines" from each ingredient. Add the heading *We're Cookin' with the Writing Process!*

 **MATERIALS**

- ❂ black butcher paper
- ❂ orange, yellow, and white construction paper
- ❂ five empty food containers

Another Idea: Change the heading to *Your Story Is the "Cat's Meow"!* Hang student-written stories around the cat.

Gold background ❖ Orange/Black Cat Cut-Outs used as border (CTP 4863)

Purr-fect Penmanship!

Enlarge, trace, color, and cut out the Cat and staple it to the center of a bulletin board titled *Purr-fect Penmanship!* Invite each student to choose a favorite handwriting sample and staple it to the board.

MATERIALS

✪ Cat *(page 211)*
✪ *handwriting samples*

Patchwork Poetry

Quilting Square background (see activity directions)

Patchwork Poetry

Invite each student to think of an object that represents himself or herself and write its name in the blank on the top of a Quilting Square. Have students use art supplies to draw a picture of the object in the center of the square and complete the sentence on the right side. Hang the quilting pieces on a bulletin board and add the title *Patchwork Poetry*.

 **MATERIALS**

✪ Quilting Square (page 212)

✪ art supplies

Another Idea: Hang a labeled manila envelope for each student. Have students write letters to each other and place them in the envelopes. Change the heading to *Classroom Postal Service*.

Gold background ✤ Patriotic Decor border (CTP 0348)

Stamp of Approval

Enlarge, trace, color, and cut out the Mailbox and staple it to a bulletin board titled *Stamp of Approval*. Invite each student to select one person he or she believes should be honored by being featured on a postage stamp. Have students write a letter to the U.S. Postal Service that nominates the person and explains why he or she should be chosen. Invite students to design on construction paper a stamp featuring the person. Hang the letters and stamps around the mailbox. Don't forget to send the letters after the board is disassembled!

 **MATERIALS**

❂ Mailbox (page 213)
❂ writing paper
❂ construction paper

Purple background ✤ Gold Stars border (CTP 0151)

Pen Pal to the Stars!

Make a poster with a sample "friendly fan letter" and staple it to the center of a bulletin board titled *Pen Pal to the Stars!* Obtain addresses of popular children's television, music, and film performers from the Internet or magazines. Staple photos of the stars and their addresses to a bulletin board. Place a desk with writing utensils, paper, and envelopes under the bulletin board. Invite students to consult the board and write letters to their favorite stars.

MATERIALS

- ✪ poster board
- ✪ addresses and photos of popular children's television, music, and film performers
- ✪ desk, writing utensils, paper, and envelopes

Another Idea: Change the heading to *Blue-Ribbon Recipes*. Invite students and their families to make favorite foods for the class and bring in the recipes to hang on the board.

Yellow background ❧ Rainbow Ribbons border (CTP 0353)

Blue-Ribbon Reports!

Cut a large yellow butcher-paper "trophy" and staple it to the center of a bulletin board titled *Blue-Ribbon Reports!* Write students' names on pieces of thick cloth blue ribbon. Attach the ribbons to student book reports. Staple the reports around the trophy.

 **MATERIALS**

✪ *yellow butcher paper*

✪ *thick cloth blue ribbon*

✪ *student book reports*

Another Idea: Change the heading to *Baker's Dozen.* Have students draw and display pictures of sets of 13 items.

Green background ♣ Pink/Green Cupcake Cut-Outs used as border (CTP 4898)

Favorite Foods Are Fun to Fix!

Enlarge, trace, color, and cut out the Chef and staple it to the center of a bulletin board titled *Favorite Foods Are Fun to Fix!* Invite each student to glue a paper plate, plastic utensils, and a paper napkin to a piece of construction-paper to form a place setting on a "placemat." Invite each student to write the name of his or her favorite food at the top of the placemat and write a "recipe" for the food in the center of the paper plate. Hang the place settings around the chef.

 **MATERIALS**

✪ Chef (page 214)

✪ paper plates, plastic utensils, and paper napkins

✪ construction paper

Another Idea: Change the heading to *A Whale of a Job!* and display student work.

Blue background ✤ Under the Sea border (CTP 0114) ✤ Blue/Gray Whale Cut-Outs (CTP 4886)

Whale of a Tale!

Cut out a gray butcher-paper whale and staple it to the center of a bulletin board. Invite each student to choose a favorite fiction story he or she has written and staple it to the board. Have students write their name on a paper whale cut-out and staple it to their story. Add the heading *Whale of a Tale!*

 **MATERIALS**

✪ gray butcher-paper whale

✪ favorite fiction stories written by students

✪ paper whale cut-outs

It's Smooth Sailing with This Spelling!

Vince
Cassie
Shelby
Delvin
Angie
Jacob
Kobe
Chuck
Rosie
Samuel

Another Idea: Change the heading to *Shipwrecked!* Have students write shipwreck stories and hang them near their boats.

Light Blue and Dark Blue background (see activity directions) ✤ Seashells border (CTP 0349)

It's Smooth Sailing with This Spelling!

Design a butcher-paper ocean background and staple it to a bulletin board. Add the title *It's Smooth Sailing with This Spelling!* Have each student design and cut out a paper sailboat. Invite students who achieve perfect spelling scores to staple their boat and spelling test to the bulletin board each week.

 **MATERIALS**

☢ *butcher-paper ocean background*

☢ *student-made paper sailboats*

☢ *spelling tests*

Another Idea: Change the heading to *Subtraction Is as Easy as Pie!* Have students write subtraction problems on their piece of pie before hanging.
Tan background ♣ Red Apples border (CTP 0131)

Recipe for Punctuation Pie!

Cut from butcher paper a large pie in a pie tin and attach it to a bulletin board. Add the heading *Recipe for Punctuation Pie!* Invite each student to design on construction paper a slice of pie and write on it a punctuation rule, such as *End a sentence with a period* or *Put quotation marks around spoken words.* Staple the slices around the pie.

 **MATERIALS**

✪ butcher paper
✪ construction paper

Tail-Waggin' Words!

pet fur cage fluffy dish

vet flea dig bite food

bark cat tail supper Kennel

Another Idea: Change the heading to *Dog-Gone Good Work!* Hang a work sample and a Dog reproducible for each student.

Gold background ❖ Paw Prints border (CTP 0365)

Tail-Waggin' Words!

Reproduce, color, and cut out several Dogs. Write a "word bank" word on each bone in a dog's mouth. Display the dogs on a bulletin board titled *Tail-Waggin' Words!*

 **MATERIALS**

✪ Dog (page 215)

We're Nuts about Math!

Enlarge, trace, color, and cut out a Squirrel and tape it to the classroom door. Add the title *We're Nuts about Math!* Invite each student to cut out a tan construction-paper circle and a brown construction-paper half-circle. Have students glue the half-circle on the whole circle to make an "acorn." Ask students to glue on a piece of brown yarn to make a "stem." Invite students to write their name and their favorite thing about math on the acorn. Tape the acorns to the classroom door.

 **MATERIALS**

✪ *Squirrel (page 216)*
✪ *tan and brown construction paper*
✪ *brown yarn*

Another Idea: Change the heading to *Nutritious Nuts!* Invite students to write "nut nutrition" facts on nut shapes before hanging.

Acorns border (CTP 0342)

Purple background

Guess the Shape!

Gather several round, square, rectangular, and triangular everyday objects and attach them to a bulletin board titled *Guess the Shape!* Write *circle, square, rectangle,* or *triangle* on separate index cards to match each object. Place the cards in an envelope stapled to the bulletin board. Invite students to visit the board and tack a card under each object to identify its shape.

MATERIALS

✪ several round, square, rectangular, and triangular everyday objects

✪ index cards

✪ envelope

Another Idea: Change the heading to *Time Off!* Invite each student to choose a time during the school day in which he or she wants five minutes "time off." Have students mark the time with their clocks. Give each student his or her time off when he or she behaves well in class.

Blue background ✣ Math Workout border (CTP 0110)

It's about Time!

Invite each student to use a construction-paper circle, two tagboard strips (for clock hands), and a metal brad to design a clock. Have students move their clock hands to show their favorite time of day. Ask each student to write on a slip of paper why that time of day is his or her favorite. Attach the clocks and slips of paper to a bulletin board titled *It's about Time!*

 **MATERIALS**

✪ construction-paper circles

✪ tagboard strips

✪ metal brads

✪ slips of paper

Green background ✤ Spring Blooms border (CTP 0338)

Pretty Patterns

Cut several large flower shapes from patterned fabric and wallpaper samples. Attach the flowers to a bulletin board titled *Pretty Patterns*.

 **MATERIALS**

✪ *patterned fabric and wallpaper samples*

Blue background ✤ Numbers border (CTP 0351)

One Hundred Is 100% Wonderful!

Invite students to collect in large plastic resealable bags sets of 100 small items. Attach the bags to a bulletin board titled *One Hundred Is 100% Wonderful!*

 **MATERIALS**

✪ plastic resealable bags

✪ small items (pennies, buttons, cotton swabs, toothpicks, plastic toys, etc.)

Another Idea: Change the heading to *Bear Balancing Act*. Attach to each bear equal-size bags of marbles.

Gold background ❖ Brown Bears border (CTP 0132)

Have a Look . . .

Enlarge, trace, color, and cut out three Bears. Staple the bears to a bulletin board titled *Have a Look and Take a Guess. Which Hand Is Holding More or Less?* Place three marbles in one small plastic bag and two in another. Attach each bag to the arms of a bear. Fill two bags for each remaining bear, adding more marbles to one bag in each set.

 **MATERIALS**

✪ Bear (page 165)

✪ small plastic bags

✪ marbles

Red background ❖ Ladybugs border (CTP 0355)

Ten Black Dots Can Make a Lot!

Read aloud and discuss *Ten Black Dots*. Invite each student to arrange and glue on construction paper ten black construction-paper circles to form an object. Students can outline their objects with crayons or markers. Have students write the following sentence frame under their object: *Ten black dots can make a/an (object)*. Staple the pictures to a bulletin board titled *Ten Black Dots Can Make a Lot!*

 **MATERIALS**

✪ Ten Black Dots *by Donald Crews*

✪ *black construction-paper circles*

✪ *construction paper*

Blue background ✤ Numbers border (CTP 0351)

Kids Count!

Invite each student to choose a different number and provide him or her with the corresponding cut-out numbers. Have students write their name on the cut-out(s) and decorate the number with art supplies. Tape the cut-outs in order to a bulletin board. Add the heading *Kids Count!*

 **MATERIALS**

✪ number cut-outs

✪ art supplies

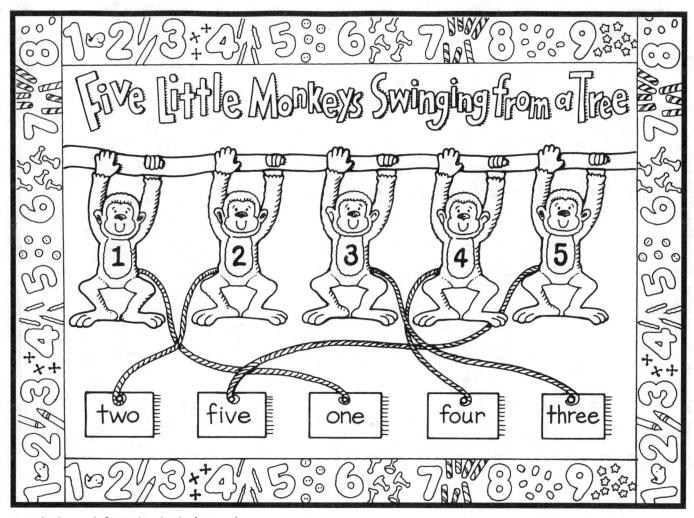

Green background ❖ Numbers border (CTP 0351)

Five Little Monkeys Swinging from a Tree

Staple a brown butcher-paper "tree branch" horizontally across a bulletin board labeled *Five Little Monkeys Swinging from a Tree*. Enlarge, trace, color, and cut out five monkeys from the Monkey reproducible. Write a number from one to five on each monkey's stomach. Staple the monkeys (in number order) to the branch so they look like they are swinging. Attach a long thick yarn "tail" to each monkey. Write a number word (from one to five) on each of five index cards and tack the cards horizontally (out of order) along the bottom of the board. Invite students to visit the board and tack each monkey's tail to its corresponding number word.

 **MATERIALS**

✪ brown butcher-paper tree branch
✪ Monkey (page 217)
✪ thick yarn
✪ index cards

Hop Aboard the " I Can Count" Train!

Black background ♣ Numbers border (CTP 0351)

Hop Aboard the "I Can Count" Train!

Enlarge, color, and cut out the engine on the Train reproducible and staple the sides and bottom of the engine (like a pocket) to the center of a bulletin board titled *Hop Aboard the "I Can Count" Train!* Invite each student to decorate a rail car. Staple the sides and bottom of each car behind the engine and number the engine and the cars in order. Write on craft sticks an ordinal number for the engine and each car. Place the craft sticks in a container near the board. Invite students to visit the board and place each craft stick in its corresponding car.

 **MATERIALS**

❂ Train (page 166)

❂ craft sticks

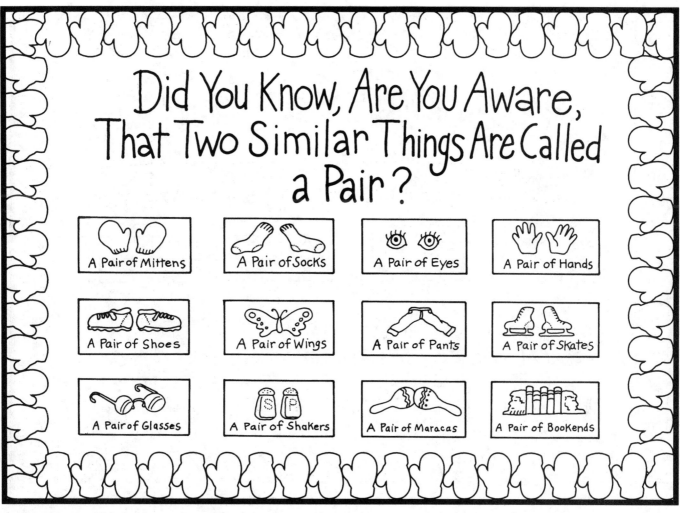

Another Idea: Change the heading to *Three Little Kittens, They Lost Their Mittens. . . .* Have students write their own version of the poem on the mitten cut-outs.

Yellow background ♣ Blue/Pink Mitten Cut-Outs used as border (CTP 4875)

Did You Know . . .

Read aloud and discuss *One, Two, One Pair*. Invite each student to draw on white construction paper a picture of something that comes in pairs. Invite each student to write *A Pair of (object name)* under his or her drawing. Staple the drawings to a bulletin board titled *Did You Know, Are You Aware, That Two Similar Things Are Called a Pair?*

 **MATERIALS**

✪ One, Two, One Pair
   by Bruce McMillan

✪ *white construction paper*

Another Idea: Change the heading to *A Bunch of Good Kids!* Make labeled "banana bunches" for student groups and hang the bunches on the bulletin board.

Blue background ❖ Yellow/Red Smiley Face Cut-Outs used as border (CTP 4873)

We're Bananas for Fractions!

Cut out several green and yellow construction-paper banana shapes. Mixing green and yellow bananas, staple bunches of bananas to a bulletin board titled *We're Bananas for Fractions!* (Be sure each bunch has a different number of bananas in it.) Write on index cards two fractions to describe the portion of yellow and green bananas in each bunch. Staple each card under its corresponding bunch.

 **MATERIALS**

✪ green and yellow construction paper
✪ index cards

Green background

It Makes Cents!

Staple several candy and food wrappers to a bulletin board. Write the price of each piece of candy or food on a separate index card and staple the cards near the wrappers. Invite students to staple the correct amount of paper-coin math manipulatives near each wrapper and card. Label the bulletin board *It Makes Cents!*

 **MATERIALS**

✪ candy and food wrappers

✪ index cards

✪ paper-coin math manipulatives

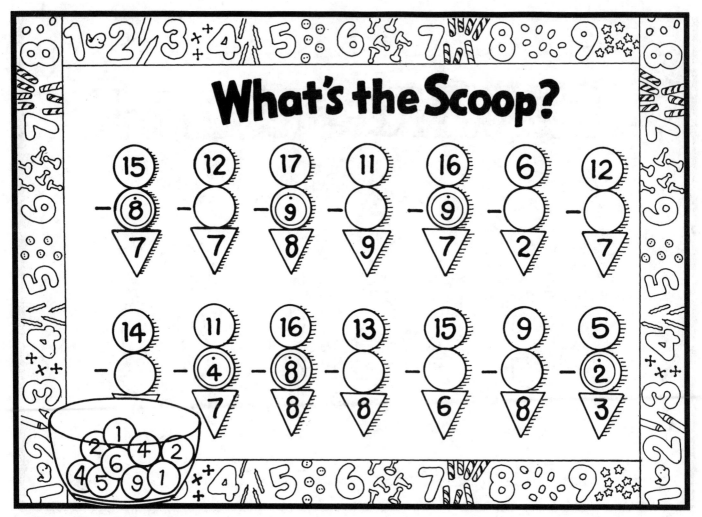

What's the Scoop?

Another Idea: Change the heading to *"Cool" Words!* Invite students to write on ice-cream scoops synonyms for *cold* or situations in which they feel cold. Yellow background ♣ Numbers border (CTP 0351)

What's the Scoop?

Color and cut out several tan construction-paper ice-cream cones and staple them on a bulletin board titled *What's the Scoop?* Cut out two construction-paper circles for each cone and attach them. Write on each top scoop the top number in a subtraction problem. Write on each cone the answer to each problem. Do not write the middle number in the bottom scoops. Write the middle numbers on individual construction-paper circles and place them in a plastic bowl near the bulletin board. Invite students to visit the board and tack the middle numbers on the correct scoops. Have students consult an answer key to self-check.

 **MATERIALS**

- ✪ tan construction paper
- ✪ construction-paper circles
- ✪ plastic bowl
- ✪ answer key

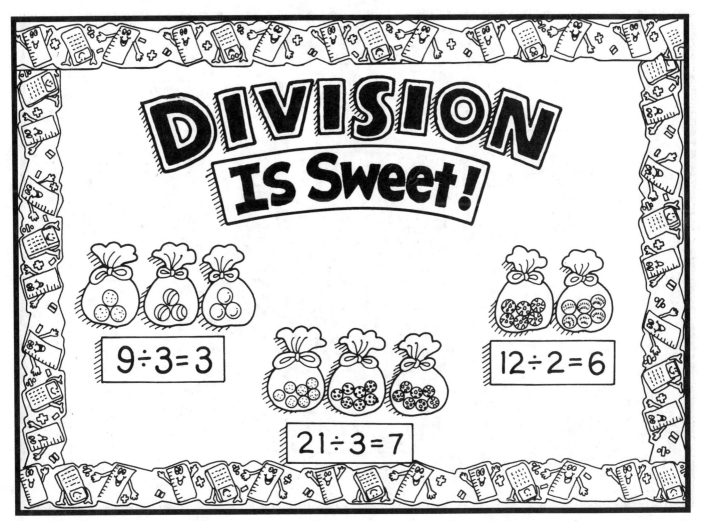

Another Idea: Change the heading to *Words to Chew On!* Write a new vocabulary word on each gum ball before attaching it to the board.

Blue background ♣ Math Workout border (CTP 0110)

Division Is Sweet!

Write three division problems on sentence strips and staple them to a bulletin board. Staple groups of construction-paper circles to the board to demonstrate each problem. Shape and staple plastic wrap over the circles so each group looks like a bag of candy. Staple a paper ribbon where each bag gathers. Label the bulletin board *Division Is Sweet!*

 **MATERIALS**

✪ *sentence strips*

✪ *construction-paper circles*

✪ *plastic wrap*

✪ *paper ribbon*

Another Idea: Change the heading to *Use Your Noodle When You Write!* Have students write punctuation and capitalization rules on paper pasta bowls. Gold background ❖ Math Workout border (CTP 0110)

Place-Value Pasta!

Staple a large butcher-paper bowl to the center of a bulletin board labeled *Place-Value Pasta!* Glue dry macaroni above the bowl so the bowl looks like it is filled with pasta. Write several numbers (without commas) with values above one thousand on separate sentence strips and staple them around the bowl. Glue individual macaroni pieces to small paper rectangles and place them in a bowl near the bulletin board. Invite students to tack the individual macaroni pieces on the numbers to show where commas should be placed. Have students consult an answer key to self-check.

 **MATERIALS**

- ✪ large butcher-paper bowl
- ✪ dry macaroni
- ✪ sentence strips
- ✪ small paper rectangles
- ✪ plastic bowl
- ✪ answer key

You Are Now Entering . . .

Invite each student to choose a favorite piece of science equipment, such as a microscope or magnifying glass. Ask each student to wear a lab coat or large white shirt and safety glasses and hold the piece of equipment as you take his or her photo with an instant camera. Tape each student's photo to the classroom door and add the heading *You Are Now Entering (Your Name's) Laboratory!*

 **MATERIALS**

✪ science equipment
✪ lab coat or large white shirt and safety glasses
✪ instant camera/film

Another Idea: Change the heading to *No "Lion," This Work Is Grrr-eat!* and attach student work samples.
Green background

We're Not "Lion," We Like Animals!

Enlarge, trace, color, and cut out the Lion and attach it to a bulletin board titled *We're Not "Lion," We Like Animals!* Invite each student to draw on construction paper and cut out a picture of his or her favorite animal. Attach the animals to the bulletin board.

 **MATERIALS**

✪ *Lion (page 187)*
✪ *white construction paper*

ANIMAL HIDE AND SEEK

Another Idea: Attach a variety of patterned wrapping paper to the bulletin board and invite students to design an imaginary animal that can be camouflaged by one of the wrapping papers.

Blue background ♣ Grass border (CTP 0359)

Animal Hide and Seek

Enlarge, trace, and cut out each animal on the Hide and Seek reproducible. Color the tiger orange and black and glue it to a piece of orange butcher paper colored with black wavy stripes. Color the chameleon red and glue it to a piece of red butcher paper. Color the walking stick brown and attach it to a brown butcher-paper "twig." Staple the camouflaged animals to a bulletin board titled *Animal Hide and Seek*.

 **MATERIALS**

✪ Hide and Seek (page 218)

✪ orange, red, and brown butcher paper

Another Idea: Change the heading to *Blooming with Knowledge!* Have students write on flowers one important thing they learned this school year.
Light Blue background ✤ Spring Blooms border (CTP 0338)

A Garden of Good Children

Cut green butcher-paper fringed "grass" and attach it to the bottom of a bulletin board titled *A Garden of Good Children*. Add a butcher-paper sun and clouds to the background. Invite each student to design a paper flowering plant and label each plant part. Glue each student's photo in the center of his or her flower and attach the plants to the bulletin board.

 MATERIALS

- ✪ green, yellow, and white butcher paper
- ✪ construction paper
- ✪ student photos

Light Blue background ❖ Butterflies border (CTP 0354)

Monarch Meadow

Create with art supplies a variety of flowers and grass and attach them to a bulletin board to make a "meadow." Invite each student to fold a piece of white construction paper in half and open it. Have students dip a hand, fingers together, thumb extended, in orange paint. Ask student to line up the painted thumb with the crease on the paper and press down to make a handprint. Have students fold the paper so the same print reproduces on the other side of the crease. Invite students to add black details so the handprints resemble a monarch butterfly. Have students cut out the butterflies and tape them to the meadow bulletin board. Add the heading *Monarch Meadow*.

 **MATERIALS**

- ✪ art supplies
- ✪ white construction paper
- ✪ orange and black tempera paint/paintbrushes

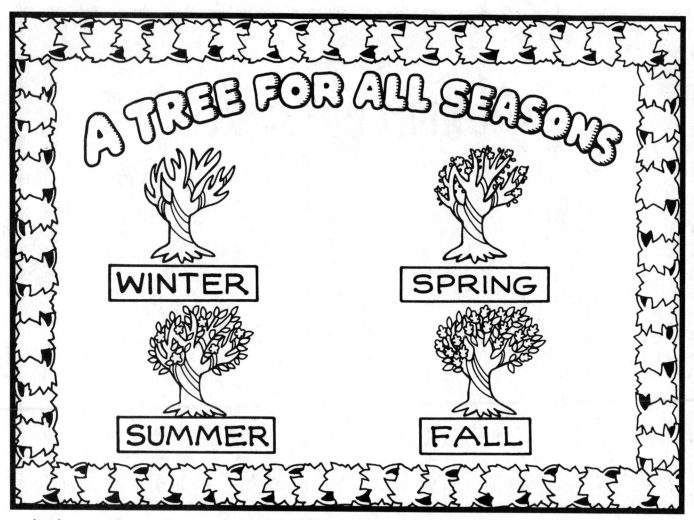

Another Idea: Have each student choose a season and draw a tree illustration to represent it. Hang the illustrations near the headings on the board. Green background ✤ Maple Leaves border (CTP 0138) ✤ Red/Yellow Autumn Leaf Cut-Outs (CTP 4885) ✤ Yellow/Purple Tulip Cut-Outs (CTP 4857)

A Tree for All Seasons

Enlarge, trace, color, and cut out four identical trees from the Tree reproducible. Divide a bulletin board into four sections and staple each tree in a section. Title the board *A Tree for All Seasons*. Label each tree with a season: *Winter, Spring, Summer, Fall*. Leave the "winter tree" bare. Attach small plastic flower and leaf buds to the "spring tree." Cover the "summer tree" with green paper leaves and flower cut-outs. Attach real fall leaves to the "fall tree."

 **MATERIALS**

✪ Tree (page 219)

✪ small plastic flowers and leaves

✪ green paper leaf and flower cut-outs

✪ real fall leaves

Blue background ✤ Garden Creatures border (CTP 0145)

Insects Are "Pop"ular!

Invite each student to use chalk and a 9" x 12" (23 cm x 30.5 cm) piece of construction paper to make a drawing of an insect. Have students fill in their drawings and the background with glued-on pieces of colored popcorn kernels to make mosaics. Staple the mosaics to a bulletin board titled *Insects Are "Pop"ular!* Staple a 12" x 18" (30.5 cm x 46 cm) piece of construction paper over each drawing to become a "pop out" frame. Cut an *X* in each frame, cutting from the center to approximately 1" (2.5 cm) from the end of each of its four corners. Fold back the four triangle flaps created by the cuts and staple them to the bulletin board so the frame pops out.

 **MATERIALS**

❂ chalk

❂ 9" x 12" (23 cm x 30.5 cm) pieces of construction paper

❂ colored popcorn

❂ 12" x 18" (30.5 cm x 46 cm) pieces of construction paper

THE EARTH IS...

The Earth is a planet.

The Earth is full of life.

The Earth is a sphere.

The Earth is "the water planet."

The Earth is hot inside.

The Earth is in space.

The Earth is old.

The Earth is big.

The Earth is shaken by earthquakes.

The Earth is not flat.

The Earth is changing.

The Earth is revolving.

The Earth is spinning.

The Earth is beautiful.

Blue and Green Construction-Paper background (see activity directions) ✤ Fragile Earth border (CTP 0252)

The Earth Is . . .

Staple pieces of blue and green construction paper alternately to a bulletin board to create a "checkerboard" background. (Be sure there is a piece for each student.) Invite each student to paint the ocean and continents on a large paper plate to represent the earth. Have students complete the sentence *The Earth is_____* on a slip of paper. Ask students to glue the paper on their plate. Attach the plates to the bulletin board and add the heading *The Earth Is. . . .*

 MATERIALS

- ✪ blue and green construction paper
- ✪ paper plates
- ✪ tempera paint/paintbrushes
- ✪ slips of paper

Another Idea: Change the heading to *Windy Words!* Invite students to write on the clothes words that remind them of the wind.

Light Blue background ❖ Clouds and Kites border (CTP 0346)

Wind Is Air In Motion!

Invite each student to design on construction paper an article of clothing, such as a shirt, pair of pants, sock, or jacket. Ask students to cut out the clothing and color both sides. Hang a piece of string across a bulletin board and paper clip each article of clothing to the string to represent a clothesline. Bend and fold the clothing so it looks like it is blowing in the wind. Add the heading *Wind Is Air In Motion!*

 **MATERIALS**

✪ construction paper

✪ string

✪ paper clips

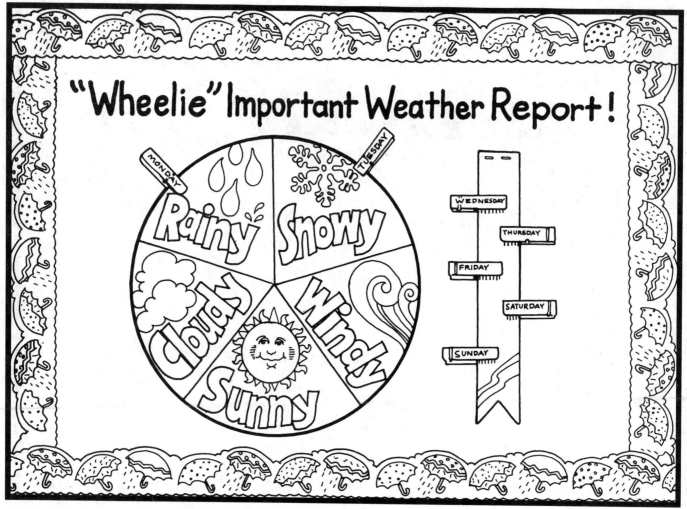

Light Blue background ♣ Umbrellas border (CTP 0337)

"Wheelie" Important Weather Report!

Enlarge, trace, color, and cut out the Weather Wheel and staple it to a bulletin board titled *"Wheelie" Important Weather Report!* Write the name of each day of the week on a separate clothespin and attach the clothespins to a cloth ribbon. Staple the ribbon next to the weather wheel. Each day, invite a volunteer to attach a clothespin to the weather wheel to show the weather for the day.

 **MATERIALS**

✪ *Weather Wheel (page 220)*

✪ *clothespins*

✪ *cloth ribbon*

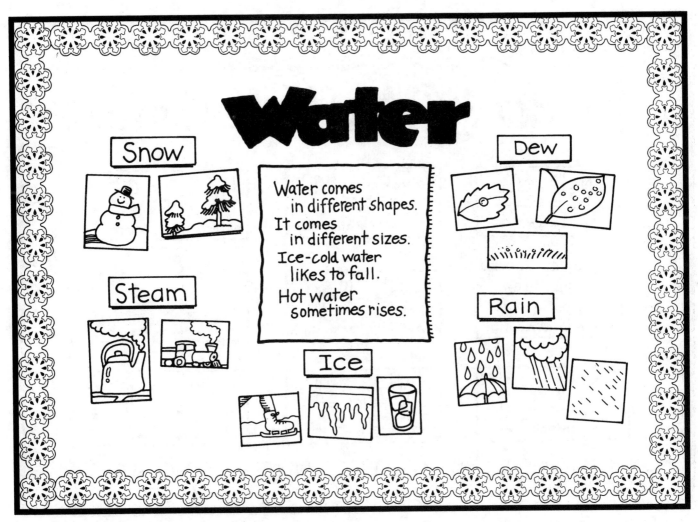

Blue background ✤ Ice Crystals border (CTP 0142)

Water

Write the following poem in the center of a piece of butcher paper:

Water comes in different shapes.
It comes in different sizes.
Ice-cold water likes to fall.
Hot water sometimes rises.

Staple the poem in the center of a bulletin board titled *Water*. Write *Snow, Ice, Steam, Dew,* and *Rain* on individual sentence strips and staple them around the poem. Invite each student to draw on construction paper a picture of one form of water and staple the picture near the word that best describes its subject.

 **MATERIALS**

✪ *butcher paper*
✪ *sentence strips*
✪ *construction paper*

I'm "Handy"! My Hands Can...

My hands can draw. — Natalie

My hands can write. — Ty

My hands can hold scissors. — Angie

My hands can clean up. — Luke

My hands can touch. — Paul

My hands can vacuum. — Jason

My hands can sweep. — Lizzy

My hands can type. — Sarah

My hands can catch balls. — Nick

Another Idea: Change the heading to *Wash Your Hands and. . . .* Invite students to write personal-hygiene tips near their handprints.

Red background ✤ Brown/Tan Handprint Cut-Outs used as border (CTP 4866)

I'm "Handy"! My Hands Can . . .

Invite students to paint their palms and press them onto construction paper. Ask students to name one thing they can do with their hands and write the answer under their handprints. Attach the handprints to a bulletin board titled *I'm "Handy"! My Hands Can. . . .*

 **MATERIALS**

✪ *construction paper*

✪ *tempera paints/paintbrushes*

Blue background ❧ White/Pink Tooth Cut-Outs (CTP 4871)

Brushing Each Day Keeps the Dentist Away!

Cut a large toothbrush and tube of toothpaste from butcher paper, decorate them, and staple them to the center of a bulletin board titled *Brushing Each Day Keeps the Dentist Away!* Write each student's name on a plastic cup and attach each cup to the bulletin board. Invite students to floss at home each night and then bring in (the next day) a short note from a family member confirming that they flossed. For each returned note, invite students to place a paper tooth cut-out in their cup. When a student has ten teeth in his or her cup, reward the student with a toothbrush or small box of dental floss.

 **MATERIALS**

- ✪ *butcher paper*
- ✪ *plastic cups*
- ✪ *paper tooth cut-outs*
- ✪ *toothbrushes or small boxes of dental floss*

Gold background ♣ Heart Cookies border (CTP 0345)

Exercise Is "Heart Smart"!

Attach a red butcher-paper heart to the center of a bulletin board and write inside it *Exercise Is "Heart Smart"!* Invite each student to draw a picture of himself or herself participating in an athletic activity and write *I (heart drawing) (activity)* on the picture. Attach the pictures to the bulletin board.

 **MATERIALS**

✪ *red butcher-paper heart*

✪ *drawing paper*

We Are a Community!

 Take photos of groups of students playing together, working together, and helping each other. Tape each photo to the classroom door and attach a sentence strip that describes each activity, such as *We play together*. Add the heading *We Are a Community!*

MATERIALS

⊛ *camera/film*

⊛ *sentence strips*

Another Idea: Have students write thank-you notes to community helpers and hang them near the corresponding hats on the bulletin board before delivering them.

Blue background

Hats Off to Community Helpers!

Enlarge, trace, color, and cut out the Hats and staple them to a bulletin board titled *Hats Off to Community Helpers!* Use a sentence strip to label the job performed by a person who wears each hat. Place a coat tree near the bulletin board and hang several real career hats on the tree. Invite students to try on the hats.

✋ **MATERIALS**

✪ *Hats (page 221)*

✪ *coat tree*

✪ *real career hats*

Another Idea: Change the heading to *A View of the Past*. Invite students to draw and display "snapshots" of times long ago.
White background ❖ Brown Bears border (CTP 0132)

Super Snapshots: A Trip to (the Zoo)!

Invite each student to draw on white construction paper a favorite scene or experience from a recent field trip. Cut four black construction-paper triangles for each student and glue the triangles to the corners of the drawings so the drawings resemble photographs. Invite each student to write on a slip of paper a description of the "snapshot." Display the snapshots on a bulletin board titled *Super Snapshots: A Trip to (field trip location)!*

 **MATERIALS**

✪ *white construction paper*

✪ *black construction-paper triangles*

✪ *slips of paper*

Light Blue and Green background (see activity directions) ✤ Fragile Earth border (CTP 0252)

Welcome to Our Community

Cover a bulletin board with light blue butcher paper and add cotton-ball clouds. Add crumpled green butcher paper to the bottom of the board to represent land. Invite each student to decorate a small box to represent a building in your community, such as a school, the city hall, or a movie theater. Attach the boxes to the green paper so they are resting on the "land." Add the title *Welcome to Our Community*.

 **MATERIALS**

✪ *light blue and green butcher paper*
✪ *cotton balls*
✪ *small boxes*

Blue background

Alpena Is Awesome

Title a bulletin board with an alliterative title that includes your community's name, such as *Alpena Is Awesome, Lovely La Grange,* or *Celebrate Cypress*. Obtain community brochures and maps from the local Chamber of Commerce and areas of interest, and if you live in a tourist destination, obtain postcards and souvenirs from local gift shops. Staple the information to the bulletin board.

 **MATERIALS**

✪ brochures and maps from the local Chamber of Commerce and areas of interest

✪ postcards and souvenirs from local gift shops

Reproducible Pattern background (see activity directions)

We Need Transportation to "Get Up and Go"!

Enlarge, trace, color, and cut out the Background and staple it to a bulletin board titled *We Need Transportation to "Get Up and Go"!* Then invite each student to design on construction paper and cut out a form of air, water, or land transportation to add to the background. (Be sure to discuss the concepts of size and scale before having students design their forms of transportation.) Attach the transportation cut-outs to the background.

 **MATERIALS**

✪ Background (page 222)

✪ construction paper

Everyone Communicates!

1. Signing
2. Reading Braille
3. Writing
4. Using the Telephone
5. Sending Morse Code
6. Using Flags on Ships
7. Drawing Pictographs
8. Singing
9. Sending Signals with Flares
10. Using Radar

Another Idea: Invite students to draw and display illustrations of how they communicate with others, such as through body language, speech, or sounds.

Yellow background ✤ Happy Notes border (CTP 0242)

Everyone Communicates!

Enlarge, trace, color, and cut out the ten boxes on the Forms of Communication reproducible. Staple the pictures to a bulletin board. Title the bulletin board *Everyone Communicates!*

 **MATERIALS**

✪ *Forms of Communication (page 223)*

Art Gallery

Invite each student to design a miniature watercolor painting on half of an index card. Mount the paintings on construction-paper rectangles and tape them to your classroom door. Add the heading *Welcome to Mr./Ms. _____'s Art Gallery!*

MATERIALS

✪ *watercolor paints/paintbrushes*
✪ *3" x 5" (7.5 cm x 12.5 cm) blank index cards*
✪ *construction-paper rectangles*

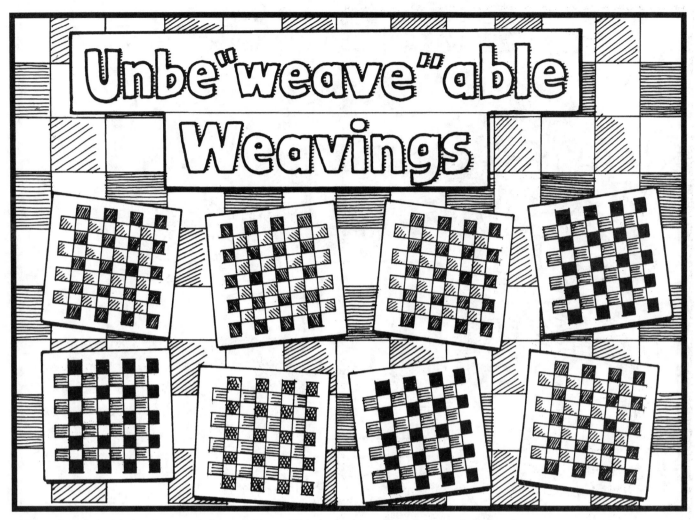

Another Idea: Change the heading to *Unbe"weave"able Work!* Display student work on the woven background.

Blue Woven background (see activity directions)

Unbe"weave"able Weavings

Cut horizontal slits through a large blue butcher-paper background so the slits end approximately 2" (5 cm) from each end. Weave several thick butcher-paper strips through the background to create a giant weaving. Attach the weaving on the bulletin board. Mount student-made weavings to black construction-paper "frames" and attach the frames to the bulletin board. Add the heading *Unbe"weave"able Weavings*.

 MATERIALS

- ✪ blue butcher paper
- ✪ colored butcher-paper strips
- ✪ student-made weavings
- ✪ black construction paper

Blue background ♣ Kids of the World border (CTP 0143)

A World of Many Faces!

Invite students to observe in books masks from around the world. Have each student make a mask that represents a different country. Attach an elastic band to each mask. Hang a mirror in the center of a bulletin board. Tack the masks around the mirror so they hang by their bands. Add the heading *A World of Many Faces!* Invite students to visit the bulletin board and try on the masks.

 MATERIALS

- ✪ books with masks from around the world
- ✪ mask-making supplies
- ✪ elastic bands
- ✪ mirror

Green background ♣ Brown/Tan Boy Cut-Outs (CTP 4933) ♣ Brown/Tan Girl Cut-Outs (CTP 4934)

Super Shelves

Invite each student to decorate a shoe-box top with wrapping paper. Staple the box tops upside down to a bulletin board so they resemble shelves. Write each student's name on a boy or girl cut-out and tape the cut-out to his or her box. Add the heading *Super Shelves*. Invite students to place on the shelves favorite lightweight projects, collections, or sculptures for a delightful 3-D display.

 **MATERIALS**

- ✪ shoe-box tops
- ✪ wrapping paper
- ✪ paper boy and girl cut-outs
- ✪ lightweight projects, collections, or sculptures

Tan background

"Dino"mite Drawings!

Enlarge a Dinosaur Peekover for each student and invite students to color and cut it out. Have students attach the peekovers to a favorite drawing. Staple the drawings to a bulletin board titled *"Dino"mite Drawings!*

 **MATERIALS**

✪ *Dinosaur Peekover (page 224)*

✪ *student drawings*

Green background

These Pictures Are "Peachy"!

Invite each student to cut out a peach-colored felt circle and write his or her name in the center. Have students add green construction-paper stems and a leaf to make a "peach." Have students attach the peach to a favorite drawing. Staple the drawings to a bulletin board titled *These Pictures Are "Peachy"!*

MATERIALS

✪ peach-colored felt

✪ green construction paper

✪ student artwork

Movie Camera

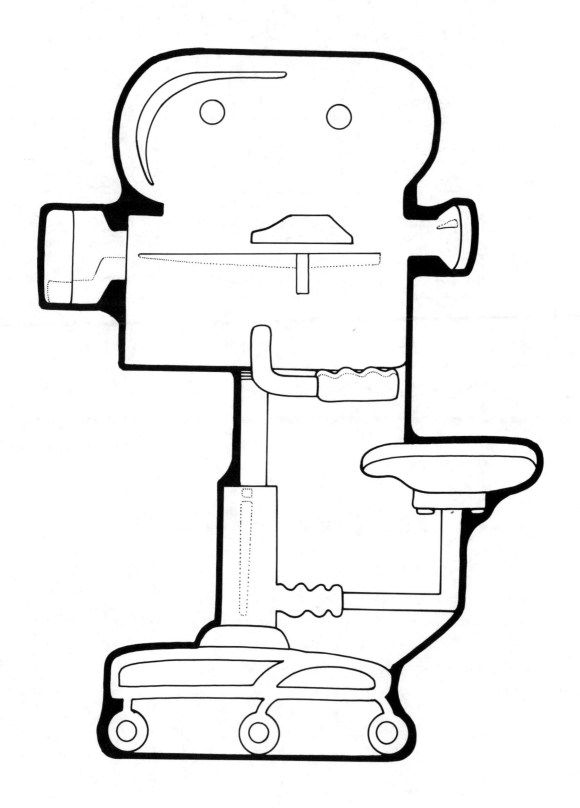

The Giant Book of Bulletin Boards © 1998 Creative Teaching Press

Bear

Train

The Giant Book of Bulletin Boards © 1998 Creative Teaching Press

Fish

Octopus

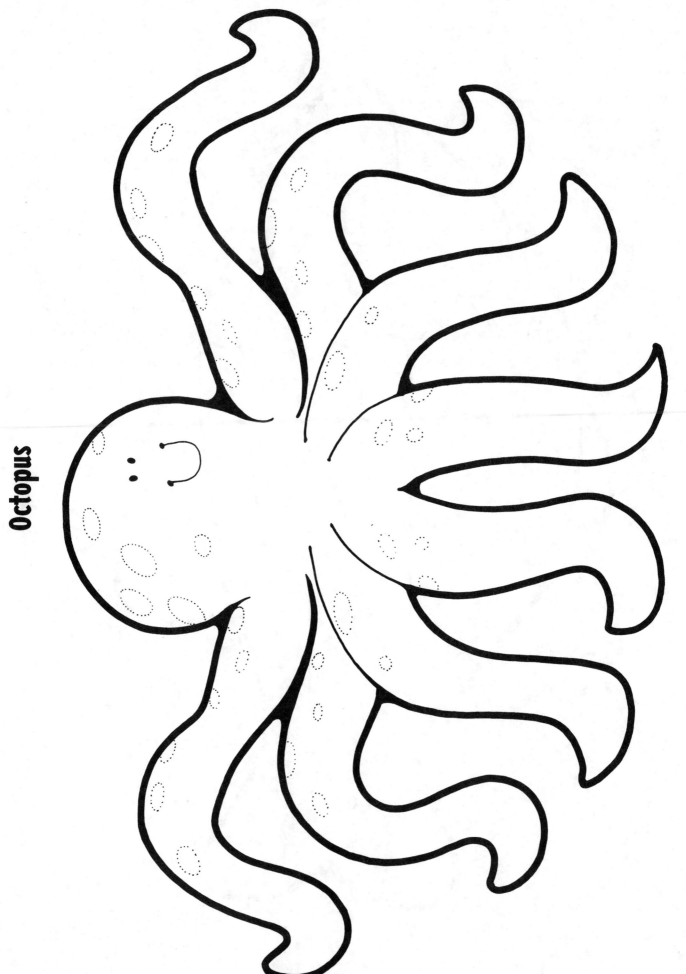

The Giant Book of Bulletin Boards © 1998 Creative Teaching Press

Clams

Tooth Fairy

The Giant Book of Bulletin Boards © 1998 Creative Teaching Press

Bus, Car, Shoe, and Bike

Scarecrow

The Giant Book of Bulletin Boards © 1998 Creative Teaching Press

Haunted House

Bat

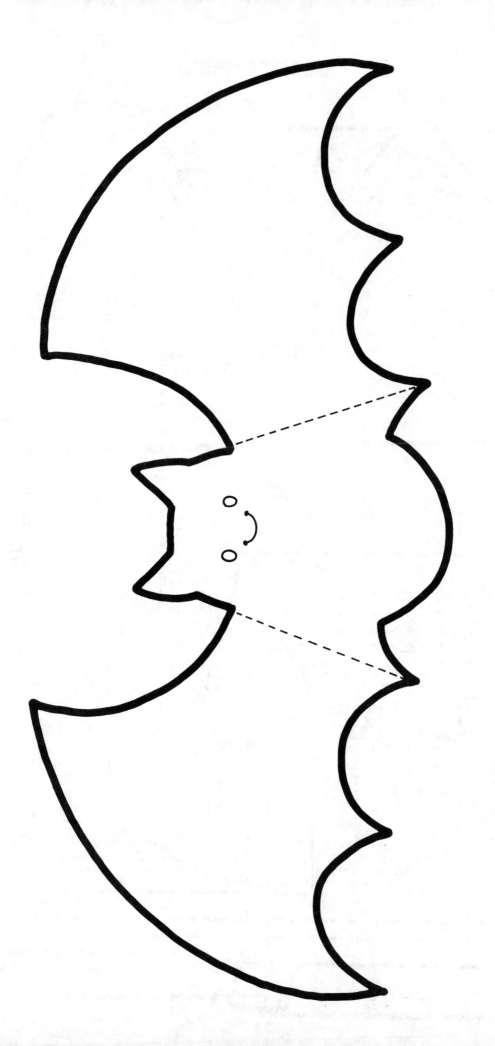

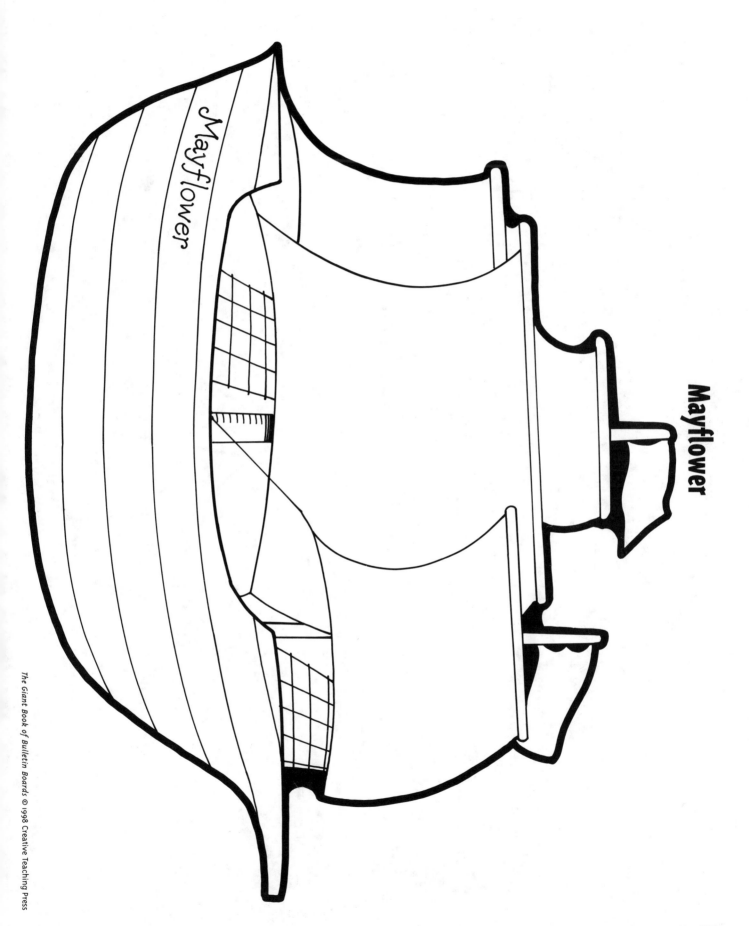

Mayflower

Mayflower

Turkey

The Giant Book of Bulletin Boards © 1998 Creative Teaching Press

Let's Talk Turkey

Gingerbread Man

Paper Doll

Bells

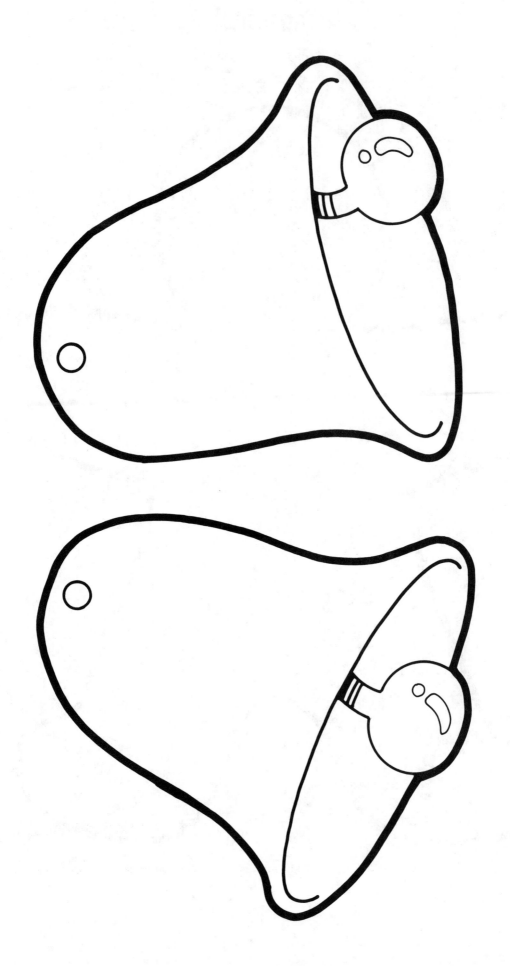

The Giant Book of Bulletin Boards © 1998 Creative Teaching Press

Menorah

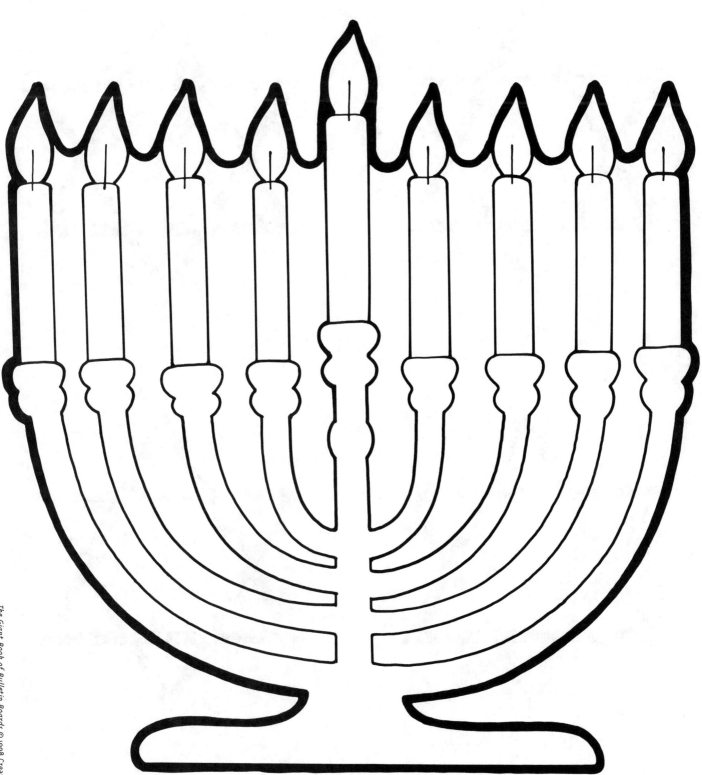

Star of David

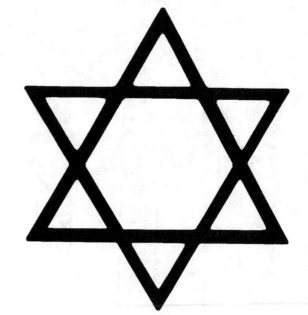

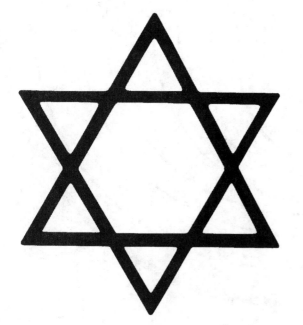

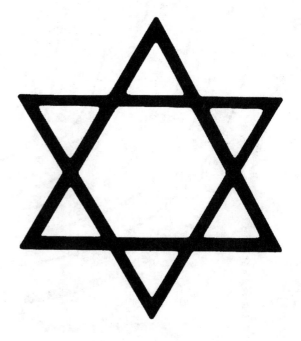

The Giant Book of Bulletin Boards © 1998 Creative Teaching Press

Martin Luther King, Jr.

"Million-Dollar President" Bills

The Giant Book of Bulletin Boards © 1998 Creative Teaching Press

Cupid

Sled

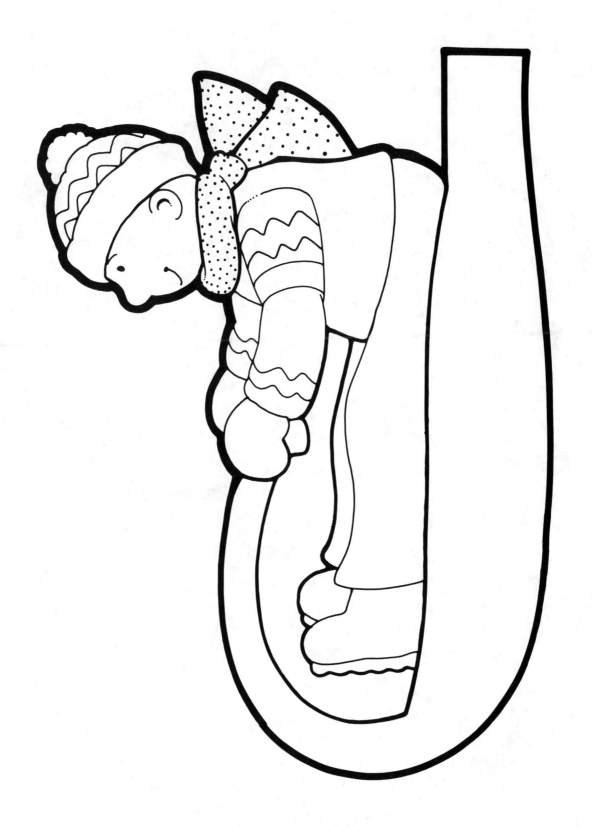

The Giant Book of Bulletin Boards © 1998 Creative Teaching Press

Lion

Lamb

The Giant Book of Bulletin Boards © 1998 Creative Teaching Press

Leprechaun

Bunny

The Giant Book of Bulletin Boards © 1998 Creative Teaching Press

Basket

Rollerblade

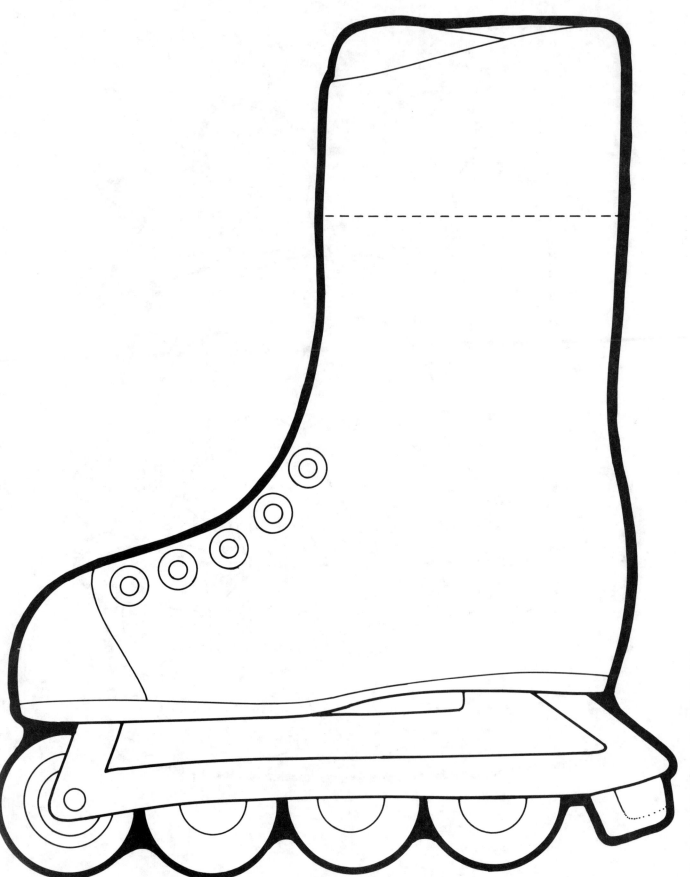

The Giant Book of Bulletin Boards © 1998 Creative Teaching Press

Horse

Bee

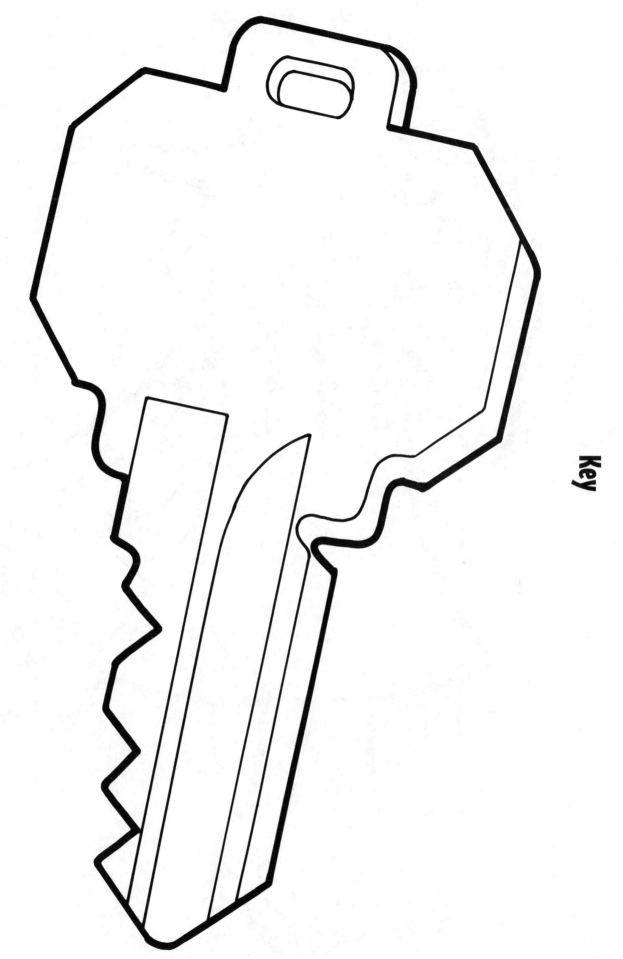

Key

The Giant Book of Bulletin Boards © 1998 Creative Teaching Press

Miss Manners

The Giant Book of Bulletin Boards © 1998 Creative Teaching Press

Balloon

Cow

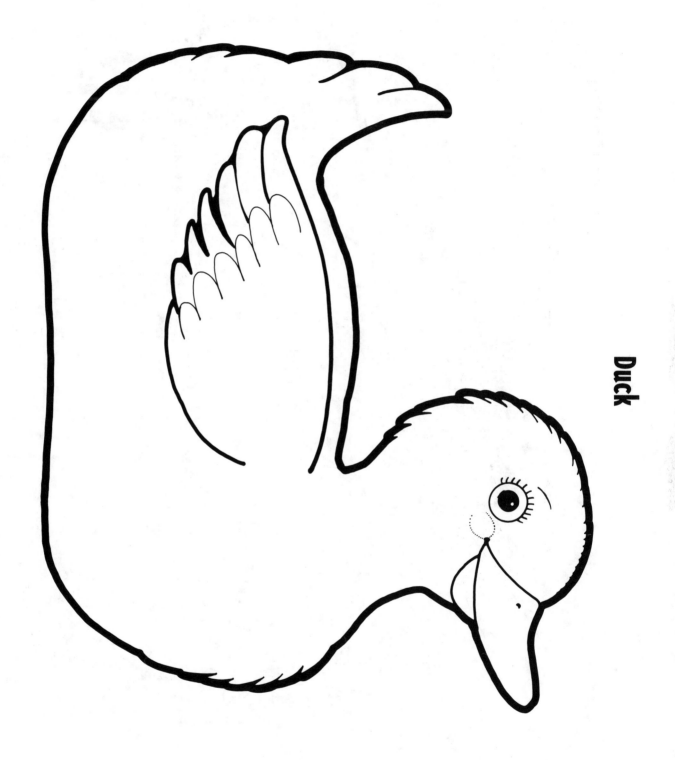

Duck

Crow

The Giant Book of Bulletin Boards © 1998 Creative Teaching Press

Dragon

Old Lady

Animals She Swallowed

fly

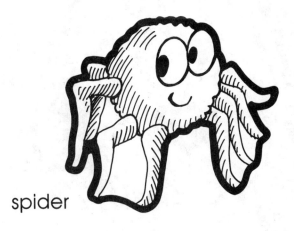

spider

bird

cat

Animals She Swallowed

dog

goat

cow

horse

Mouse and Clock

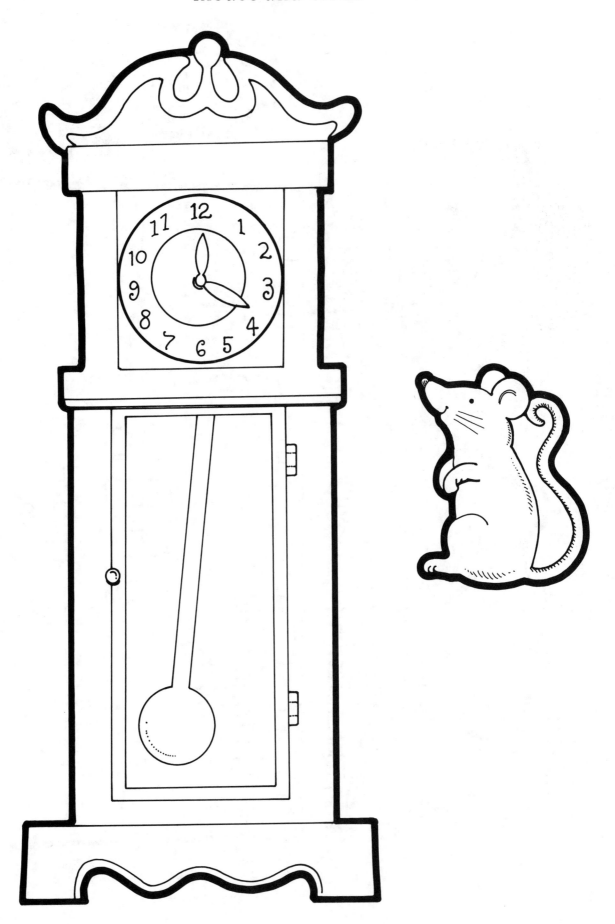

Castle and Princess

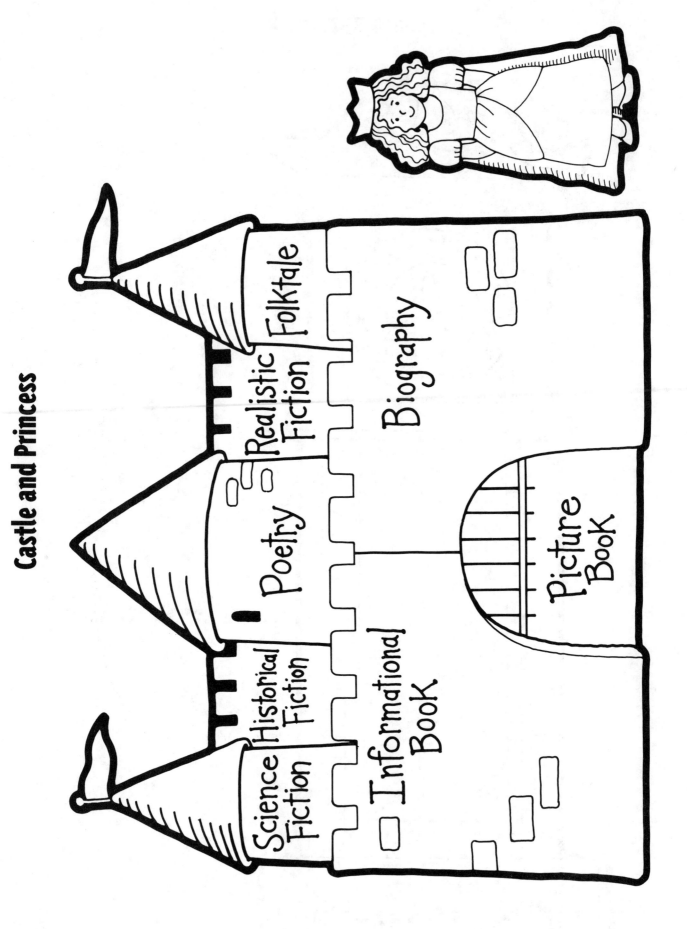

Folktale

Realistic Fiction

Biography

Poetry

Picture Book

Science Historical Fiction Fiction

Informational Book

The Giant Book of Bulletin Boards © 1998 Creative Teaching Press

Iguana

Baby

The Giant Book of Bulletin Boards © 1998 Creative Teaching Press

Pig

Pencil

The Giant Book of Bulletin Boards © 1998 Creative Teaching Press

Cat

The patches on this quilt you see
Were each made very carefully.

I drew a picture of a _____ on mine,
As you can see from this design.

I chose this picture especially—
The _____ is _____, just like me!

Mailbox

Chef

The Giant Book of Bulletin Boards © 1998 Creative Teaching Press

Dog

Squirrel

The Giant Book of Bulletin Boards © 1998 Creative Teaching Press

Monkey

Hide and Seek

chameleon

walking stick

tiger

The Giant Book of Bulletin Boards © 1998 Creative Teaching Press

Tree

Weather Wheel

Hats

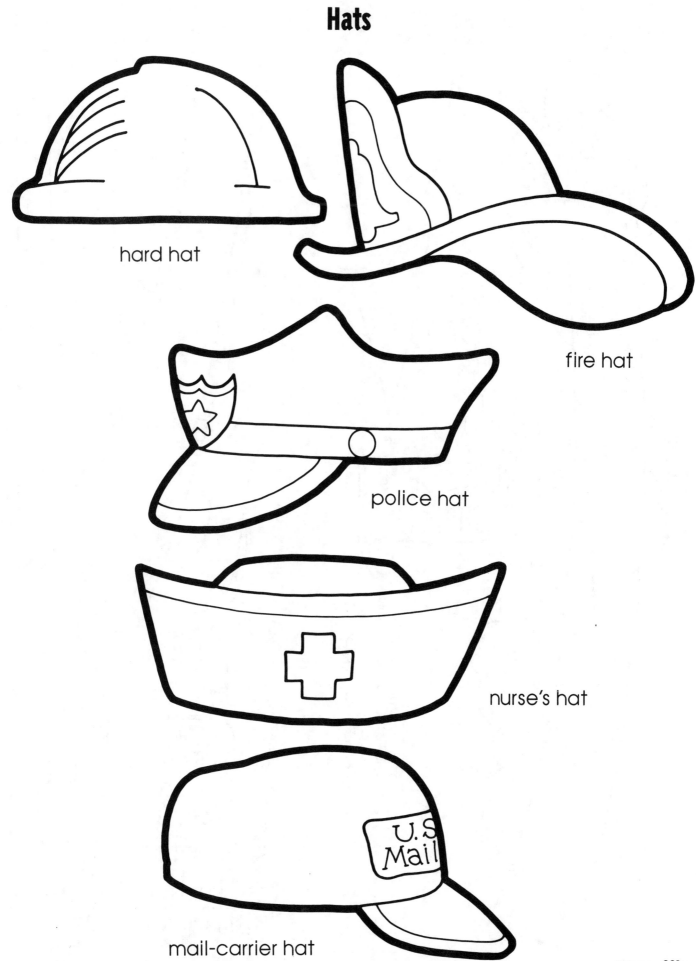

hard hat

fire hat

police hat

nurse's hat

U.S.
Mail

mail-carrier hat

Background

Forms of Communication

1. Signing

2. Reading Braille

G O

3. Writing

4. Using the Telephone

5. Sending Morse Code

S O S

6. Using Flags on Ships

H I

7. Drawing Pictographs

hunt

8. Singing

9. Sending Signals with Flares

10. Using Radar

Dinosaur Peekover

The Giant Book of Bulletin Boards © 1998 Creative Teaching Press